# SIX WEEKS
TO A
# SIMPLER LIFESTYLE

# SIX WEEKS TO A SIMPLER LIFESTYLE

Barbara DeGrote-Sorensen
and
David Allen Sorensen

SIX WEEKS TO A SIMPLER LIFESTYLE



Cover design: McCormick Creative
Interior design: James F. Brisson

---

Library of Congress Cataloging-in-Publication Data

DeGrote-Sorensen, Barbara, 1954–
Six weeks to a simpler lifestyle / by Barbara DeGrote-Sorensen and David Allen Sorensen.
p. cm.
Includes bibliographical references.
ISBN 0-8066-2751-4
1. Christian life. 2. Simplicity—Religious aspects—Christianity. 3. Life style. I. Sorensen, David Allen, 1953– . II. Title. III. Title: 6 weeks to a simpler lifestyle.
BV4501.2.D4317 1994
241'.68—dc 20 94-33426
CIP

---

The paper used in this publication meets the minimum requirements of American National Standard for Information Sciences—Permanence of Paper for Printed Library Materials, ANSI Z329.48–1984. ∞™

---

Manufactured in the U.S.A. AF 9-2751

99 98 97 96 95 1 2 3 4 5 6 7 8 9 10

ACKNOWLEDGMENTS

Some of the kindest people we have ever known have been our book developers and editors over the years:

We thank Roland Seboldt for enlisting us a decade ago to write first in the *Young Readers Series* and then the *Young Christian Series* of fiction books for pre-teens, giving us our start as authors. With equal measures of far-sighted vision and practicality, Roland is a rare asset and true patriarch of the church of Jesus Christ.

We owe a large debt to Bob Moluf for urging us to write about our journeys in life on the road to simplicity. His gentle wisdom, friendship, and guidance have been a blessing to us for a decade.

We are grateful to Cindy Nelson, Irene Getz, and John Hanka for their many hours of nursing our book manuscripts along over the years.

And we are especially delighted that Ron Klug dug into his deep spiritual center to find the space and time for us and for Augsburg books, from which we all will benefit. May it be so for many years to come!

# CONTENTS

# INTRODUCTION

# Once Upon a Midlife Crisis

Five years have passed since we threw up our hands in exasperation over our consuming excesses, our well-earned migraines, the deck of credit cards, the overscheduled schedule, and the need to buy as much house as we could mortgage with both of us working. We were in our mid-thirties then, a little precocious since most people tend to enter the reevaluation time, often called mid-life crisis, between the ages of thirty-seven and forty-two.

We didn't begin with easy, wimpy, insignificant lifestyle changes. Among other things, we immediately sold the house that was just off the golf course in the "best neighborhood" and "moved down," reducing our financial commitment for shelter by over sixty percent.

Making smart housing choices is still important to us. We now live in a splendid but very affordable 1901 house with the interior wood trim, stained-glass windows, and character that would seem excessive for us to build new. This change in our housing values—the single largest financial commitment most people make in their lives—freed up money that allowed us to make job changes as well. That, in turn, gave us considerably more time for our young family while we still had kids at home.

If we had it to do again we'd probably move a bit more slowly, giving more time to all family members for adjustment. On the other hand, there's something to be said for jumping in at the deep end of what one fears is a cold swimming pool. But the analogy breaks down. The happy results of our initial changes reminded us less of a cold swimming pool than of a heated Jacuzzi.

Then came the myriad small adjustments that really helped us evolve from reactive anticonsumers to heartfelt simplicity seekers. Our first book on this subject, *'Tis a Gift to Be Simple*, was a book of beginnings, an invitation to a simpler life, a "why to" book. In *Six Weeks to a Simpler Lifestyle* we will share with you many of the practical insights and details we've discovered that put our good intentions into effect. This one is a "how to" book. It contains a call to cut back in many ways. But for us, simplicity is more than merely cutting back. It is an intentional lifestyle that allows our real priorities to surface, giving us a better sense of how we really want to live. Following a simpler lifestyle means evaluating our priorities again and again, and then choosing, choosing, choosing so that we rise above our almost-unconscious, habitual choices.

We're still settling into simpler lives, learning daily as we practice how better to enjoy God's gift of simplicity, but also enjoying the focus and many freedoms the gift has already brought us. We are having many "Aha!" times, when good choicdes yield immediate results and the whole journey makes glorious sense. We've also learned, in retrospect, to value the times when we don't feel so good, when we are struggling to make ends meet with time, spirit, and money, when we feel "noisy" in our hearts, when we finally admit we're overwhelmed and overextended. If we didn't have such intense feelings, why else would we change?

Movie theaters sell lots of salty popcorn to make the customers also long to buy refreshing drinks. Isn't it possible—even likely—that the Holy Spirit uses our longings and discomforts to call us to wholeness? *We have come to realize that discomfort is sometimes the gift of the Holy Spirit to move us to a finer place.* If you are unhappy with aspects of your life right now, praying for something better, you might consider that unhappiness to be a gift before the gift. *A longing heart is an appropriate beginning to a simpler life.*

Only God can create a salty heart that longs for refreshment. And only God can offer the gift of simplicity to those who sense their need. We can't initiate this grace, this unmerited gift. But we can respond to it. From a simple mumbled "thank-you" to an exuberant selling of all we have and sharing with others in need (Acts 4:32-35), we can respond to God's grace with lives which, in a simple and direct way, give glory and thanks to God.

David shares:

*I'm grateful to Barbara for inviting me (read "dragging me") into this adventure in simplicity. After my initial anxieties, it has proved to be both a genuine delight and a pleasing challenge. But at times we must shake our heads at our continued obstinacy, because in some ways we still don't "get it." We continue to hold back from giving God our whole selves, time, and possessions. It's as if we're saying, "We'll change how we live and respond out of thanks to you, Lord, but only to a certain point. . . ." Alas, I fear it will always be thus. We can be paging through our first book on simplicity at times, see something insightful (Barbara wrote all the really good parts), and say to each other, "Hey, this looks like a good idea; we really ought to try this." Then we laugh.*

*Very sincerely, we feel a bit hypocritical writing the books on simplicity and being introduced as the "lifestyle experts" at speaking engagements, at retreats, and on radio talk shows. We know we are just stumbling pedestrians on the meandering paths of simplicity. But then we take a look back to see where we have walked together in recent years, and we see how far we have come. It really is happening. We really have newer, healthier lives . . . for as much as we have allowed ourselves to receive the freeing gift of simplicity. Sure, we could hold off on writing or talking about lifestyle changes until we are really pulled together, but, friend, the book never would get written. And if that was required by the world's publishers, there wouldn't be very many other books to read, would there? We'd rather write the book now—incomplete as this process is—even if it means we must set aside the term "experts" in favor of "fellow travelers."*

*The path we've walked has been a surprising joy, but that does not mean it always has been easy. I gave up a job that I loved because it had me all over the map as a church consultant and troubleshooter with a couple hundred congregations. I woke up many days before anyone else in the family, took off to meetings all over northwestern Wisconsin, and arrived home after the kids had gone to bed. Barbara, ever the seat of wisdom in this family, said one day, "You're gone so much that one day our young children will be graduated and gone and you'll wonder what happened to them." She was right. I wasn't a very good father those days. It is much, much better now.*

*So there have been changes that entailed some inner struggles. I had to get my ego out of the way to resign from a job that gave me a lot of enjoyment and strokes. But the benefit to me, to us, to the whole family, has been even greater than we hoped it would be. I guess if reordering our priorities was easy, we could put new ones on like a new suit. But the danger would be we could also shed the good priorities too easily. It's not necessarily an easy process, but it is an important one.*

Barbara shares:

*So what have the past five years taught us? That simplicity comes in the living out of a day-to-day routine. Getting up for jobs, making beds, coming home in the evening, eating an evening meal. This is the arena in which we live and make our choices.*

*I haven't always felt successful in our quest to live out our priorities in a more integrated way. There have been days that have been more chaotic than I like. But overall, I look at the whole thing and still say, "It is good." We've gained energy for what is important to us. We hear the world news in the evening and take time to care about people we've never met. We really listen to our children's stories with our full attention and we laugh a lot more than we used to. Sometimes the dishes pile up or the evening gets late with unfinished work. I still feel the tug to replace something old with something new just for the sake of newness. But overall, the pressure's off. That inner frantic voice has been mostly calmed. I think we're learning to live with some grace in our lives. And that's God's doing. Would I go back? Not on your life.*

We have gained so much in the writing of these two books. We thank you and the other readers for making a market for them. Without other longing hearts they would not have been written and we would not have been caused to study, focus, and stretch as we have.

Finally, we thank God for stirring us to have simpler hearts, hearts that have learned the Spirit's ways to filter out some of the "noise" of our culture and center on God's grace. God is raising us out of inner relative poverty into more meaningful lives.

Journey with us for the next six weeks or so. "May the God of hope fill you with all joy and peace as you trust in him, so that you may overflow with hope by the power of the Holy Spirit." (Rom. 15:13, NIV).

*Soli Deo gloria*; to God alone the glory.

## CHAPTER 1

# You Picked Up This Book for a Reason!

Stop for a moment and ask yourself what it was about this book that caused you to take it in your hands and open it. Say it out loud, if you must, in order to remember this thought. You picked up this book for a reason, and it would be good for you to become very open and familiar with that reason.

Chances are very good that there is either a pressing, current need or the haunting, familiar echo of a longing that has rumbled around inside you for years. You may be overwhelmed, overinvolved, overextended. You are seeking a simpler life. And six weeks sounds like a reasonable amount of time in which some benefit could be gained. A month and a half. Sounds as though it would require some commitment—not a quick fix—but it's not forever.

### It isn't just you

Pick out a magazine at the newsstand or grocery store. The symptoms are all there. Recent article titles sketch a society out of sync with health, common sense, and deeper priorities:

"Instant Relief for Work Stress"

"Melt Away Holiday Stress"

"26 Simple Ways to Change the Way You Feel"

"Find Your Personal Peace: 90 Tranquility Zones for thc 90s"

"Calm Down, Slim Down: 10 'Miracle Workers' for the Overweight & Overwhelmed"

"Too Tired for Sex? Surprise Advice for Working Couples"

"The Witching Hour: It's complete chaos when you get home from work—but you can change that"

"Kid Consumers: How to make sure they buy smart"

"Getting Kids Off the Fast Track: How one family learned to slow down and savor being together"

"School Stress: Expert advice on helping your kids handle the pressure"

"Stress Signals: If you've got stomach trouble or persistent pimples, your body may be telling you to slow down"

"Calming Jangled Nerves: Six strategies for taming the stress beast"

"21 Ways to Cope with Stress"

"Dealing with the Deadline Disorder"

"The Food-Stress Link"

"Outsmarting Stress: The latest on conditioning yourself to relax when you need to"

And "On Wasting the Best Years of Our Lives"

It's not just you. It's this whole society of people who reinforce fouled-up values in each other. "You've gotta have it all, do it all, indulge your every whim, then borrow some more and party."

One recent book, *Baby Boomer Blues* by Dr. Gary Collins and Dr. Timothy Clinton, deals with the changing times of people born between 1946 and 1964. In that book, they quote Mike Bellah regarding baby boomers who, with their children, now constitute about one-half of our nation's population: "Never in the history of our country has a generation been taught to expect more from life. Never has a generation been more disappointed and disillusioned as adults." As a result of this kind of disillusionment, many are seeking greater depth and meaning in their lives. As members of this group deal with their downscaled dreams, overstretched budgets, and stalled-out careers, the sheer numbers of these consumers inevitably draw attention to their concerns.

But it isn't only the baby boomers who are grabbed by the need to live more meaningful, spiritual lives than is offered by society at large. John Naisbitt and Patricia Aburdene have predicted in their book *Megatrends 2000: Ten New Directions for the 1990s* that one of the top ten trends in America for the

1990s is religious revival. Look for a massive shift in priorities as the decadent 1980s become a dim memory and people search for more depth and meaning in their lives.

Transitions can happen at any age, causing a time of re-evaluation of one's lifestyle. Often, these transitions begin with some kind of "marker event." Someone turns 30, or 40, or 65. Someone else becomes ill or loses a spouse. Retirement. A new child. Divorce. Loss of job or income. Getting married. Getting a new job. Moving to another state. All these are prime times, when an honest soul can begin to long once again for a simpler, more integrated life.

David shares:

*I once met a man who went through an almost unbelievable transition. Though you and I aren't likely ever to go through what he did, his experience could be a model for us all on how to survive an unplanned time of change.*

*The man's twelve-year-old daughter—we'll call her Anne—had visited the church where I was working. It fell to a team of three of us to visit the homes of recent visitors, so we went calling on a Wednesday evening. Only the father was home. We tried the next week. Same thing. And the third week was no different except that the father apologized for our bad luck. Our guidelines dictated that we not go back a fourth week, but something drew us back one last time to seek out Anne.*

*She met us at the door with wide eyes and a simple "Come in. My dad's going to want to talk with you."*

*She led us through the darkened living room to the dining room. A single hanging light over the table illuminated Anne's mother and father and three blond sisters, all wearing the same grim expression as Anne.*

*"I can't believe you've come back again," her father said. "Sit down; we need to talk." We sat. "Did you hear the news story about the man who fell off a ten-story construction site this week and survived without a broken bone?" He pointed to his upper body brace. "That man was me. I remember the moment when I realized that I would certainly fall. I looked down and saw a car below me and out a bit, so I pushed off just slightly. I landed on the roof of the car, caving it in. I hurt today, but I didn't even break a bone. I guess we've all*

*gotten quite a scare. I think we're ready to talk with you about God, if that's OK."*

*By the end of the hour, all bowed our heads and shared an opportune prayer of thanks in the midst of that family's incredible transition.*

*We go through changes and transitions that are just as inevitable at some point as a man falling off a building. Something happens over which we have very little control. But just like Anne's father, we have* some *control. We may not be able to choose whether or not to go through the transition, but we* can *make choices that are life-giving, nonetheless. And we have found that transitions and life crises tend to cry out for a simpler, more focused way of dealing with things that are relatively more important.*

You picked up this book for a reason. Probably a good reason, though it may be buried so deep that you can't articulate it. Yet. We can help with that. We've been talking the language of simplicity with people for years now, and we are finding that it is anything but an esoteric language better left to the theologians and aging hippies. Simplicity is a language that probably is native born in us all. The Spirit of God has been whispering his vocabulary to us for a lifetime. Problem is, we haven't been listening. Until now. We run ourselves ragged in unnecessary complexity and in secret duplicity as we try to serve God *and* mammon, God *and* runaway career, God *and* things.

Longing for some changes? It's not just you. Blame it on the sinful human heart that is in us all. Don't be ashamed that you are feeling as you do. Be glad! Your acknowledgment of your longings is the first step in a very important journey toward a simpler life in which you can serve one God instead of many.

Do you still remember the reason you picked up this book? The reason you were supposed to speak out loud, if necessary, just to remember it? That reason—whatever it is—is your ticket into a new direction in life. That's all it takes: a longing for change because things have not lined up in life the way they were supposed to. Maybe you have a nagging feeling that there should be something more to life. Maybe you recently read Ps. 51:17: "The sacrifices of God are a broken spirit; a broken and contrite heart, O God, you will not despise" (NIV).

Come to the Lord with your life's aches, bruises, disappointments, confusions, and guilt. God's Word says, "Come near to God and he will come near to you. Wash your hands, you sinners, and purify your hearts, you double-minded. Grieve, mourn and wail. Change your laughter to mourning and your joy to gloom. Humble yourselves before the Lord, and he will lift you up" (James 4:8-10, NIV).

It's humbling to admit that you have one or many needs, and that you lack more than just an oil and filter change. You need a new heart, a rebuilt engine. Frankly, it's going to take a miracle to meet your needs, to help you sort through your priorities and find the simpler life you desire. We can't do it for you, we're sorry to report. But we can introduce you to the One who can heal you as we share something of our walk with Jesus. All we ask of you is that you read with more than your mind. Set aside any double-mindedness you may have and read with your heart and spirit. Read with the knowledge that the gospel isn't just the written word; it is the living Word, which is able to "make all things new."

## CHAPTER 2

# Gauging Your Desire for Simplicity

The section of our first book on simplicity, *'Tis a Gift to Be Simple: Embracing the Freedom of Living with Less,* that has received the most comment has been the brief lifestyle survey we developed and tried on a number of groups before the book was published. Many people have told us that it helped them find the areas of their lives in which they were most out of sync with a simple life.

There also has been enough constructive criticism of our first survey in that "why to" book that we feel we are able, in this "how to" book, to develop the survey into a *better* tool for personal use and evaluation. Thanks to those who have worked with us in honing the material in this chapter, we feel the lifestyle survey below (1) clears up a few foggy meanings, (2) gives greater emphasis or weight to elements of a simpler lifestyle that are relatively more important, and (3) goes into greater detail concerning important aspects of a simpler life.

We hope and pray that the enlarged and improved version of our lifestyle survey, presented here, gives you a good idea of the general areas as well as the specific issues in which you need the most help.

### LIFESTYLE SURVEY

**DIRECTIONS:** For each of the statements below, give yourself 5, 3, 1, or 0 points in the space provided:

5 = strongly agree
3 = somewhat agree
1 = somewhat disagree
0 = strongly disagree

We realize that your responses to some of the statements could vary, depending on certain circumstances, but it is important for you to choose the *best* response available. If you are uncertain about how to respond, ask yourself what is true *most* of the time in *most* situations, then mark your response accordingly to *all* items. (NOTE: If you fail to respond to any of the statements below, they will be treated in the scoring as "strongly disagree" items whether you intended that or not, so please respond to each statement, giving yourself 5, 3, 1, or 0 points.) Follow the instructions at the end of this survey for help with scoring and interpreting the results.

## TIME MANAGEMENT

1. ☐ My daily private time is adequate.
2. *☐ I have a systematic way of getting most things done on time.
3. *☐ I use my private time as solitude rather than as an escape.
4. *☐ I can say no to people who ask me to do things when I'm already too busy.
5. ☐ I am good at delegating tasks to others as needed.
6. ☐ I don't rush too much.
7. ☐ I am seldom late to my commitments.
8. *☐ I take adequate time for things I enjoy doing.
9. ☐ I usually have enough time to do what I need and want to do.
10. ☐ I know how to prioritize my time so I give more priority to doing things that are more important.
11. ☐ I am not secretly proud of being too busy.
12. ☐ I do not have problems with procrastination.

## FAMILY AND FRIENDS

13. *☐ I spend enough time with my loved ones.
14. ☐ When I tell people "We should get together," we usually do.

15. ☐ I have gone on a (family) vacation in the past twelve months.
16. ☐ I am rarely irritable with family and friends.
17. ☐ I have about the right amount of social activities in my life.
18. *☐ I have at least one friend with whom I can share almost anything.
19. *☐ Household chores are distributed fairly among those who are able to help.
20. ☐ People close to me know that I'm longing for a simpler life.
21. ☐ I seldom blame others for things that are my fault.
22. *☐ My family and friends support me when I want to make a change in my life.
23. *☐ I grew up in a family that valued being together.
24. ☐ I can apologize to others when necessary.

## FINANCES

25. ☐ I feel in control of my/our credit card debt.
26. ☐ I/we have not taken out a consolidation loan in the past twelve months.
27. ☐ My rent/mortgage payment is fairly easy to handle.
28. *☐ The way I spend my money allows me to be generous with others.
29. *☐ I/we do not spend too much money on nonessentials.
30. *☐ I have a good grasp of my/our financial status.
31. *☐ I am a smart shopper, not an obsessive one.
32. ☐ I feel comfortable with the amount of clothing I have.
33. *☐ I feel good about the percentage of my/our income I/we give to church and other good causes.
34. *☐ I/we budget our money.
35. ☐ I/we almost never overdraw the checking account.
36. ☐ I am rarely anxious over money matters.

## PHYSICAL HEALTH

37. *☐ I get adequate weekly exercise.
38. *☐ I take enough time each day to relax.

39. ☐ I am able to maintain a healthy weight.
40. ☐ I almost never get tension headaches or migraines.
41. ☐ I get adequate sleep most nights.
42. *☐ I eat healthfully.
43. ☐ I do not get minor illnesses any more often than most.

## EMOTIONAL HEALTH

44. ☐ I almost never get sick because of emotional stress.
45. ☐ I seldom feel overly anxious.
46. ☐ I enjoy walking or spending time outdoors.
47. *☐ People who need counseling and actually *go* are winners in my eyes.
48. ☐ I choose not to turn to drugs or alcohol when I feel overwhelmed.
49. ☐ I am usually calm when I drive in traffic.
50. *☐ I let my emotions out in a healthy way rather than have them build until I explode.
51. *☐ I lighten up and have fun at least once a week.
52. ☐ I do not have nervous habits.

## SPIRITUAL HEALTH

53. *☐ I consider Jesus Christ a friend of mine.
54. *☐ I could easily identify the three most important priorities in my life.
55. ☐ I meet regularly one-on-one with a pastor or spiritual director/guide.
56. *☐ I regularly attend worship services.
57. *☐ I know the difference between my "needs" and "wants," and I indulge them accordingly.
58. *☐ I experience forgiveness and "starting over" on a regular basis.
59. *☐ I am aware of God's active presence in my life.
60. ☐ I can admit my limitations to myself and others.
61. *☐ I have a healthy daily devotional life that includes Bible reading.
62. ☐ I enjoy discussing lifestyle matters that are important to me with others.

63. ☐ I admire people who are genuinely humble.
64. *☐ I ask God for help and thank God regularly.

## GENERAL ATTITUDES

65. ☐ I seldom long to be somewhere else.
66. *☐ I am satisfied with most aspects of my life.
67. ☐ It is important for me to recycle resources where possible.
68. *☐ I know that the way I live my life has an impact on people I have never met.
69. *☐ I keep a personal journal or diary about things that are important to me.
70. ☐ I understand the value of honest commitment.
71. *☐ I consider people more important than things.
72. ☐ I can live with imperfection in myself and others.
73. *☐ People who know me consider me a giving person.
74. *☐ I see difficulties as challenges to be solved rather than as insurmountable obstacles.
75. *☐ I like to do things for others.
76. *☐ I almost never long for a more balanced life.
77. ☐ I have previously read a book encouraging a simpler lifestyle.
78. ☐ I seldom forget things.
79. ☐ I consider myself an authentic and integrated person.
80. *☐ I set goals periodically and accomplish many of them.
81. *☐ I am optimistic that things can get better in my life.
82. ☐ I like making plans for the future.
83. ☐ I enjoy reading about lifestyle issues in magazines, in books, and even in my Bible.
84. *☐ I believe that persistence—over six weeks and more—can help a lifestyle change to become a firm habit.

### Scoring Your Lifestyle Survey

To score your lifestyle survey, add up the *survey points* you assigned yourself in the lefthand column of all the statements above. Enter the *survey points* total on page 23.

Now go back over the survey and give yourself an extra *two bonus points for each* of the items marked with a "*" *only if you* *already gave yourself 5 points* (Strongly Agree) for those specially marked statements. These are items that we consider more important for you to agree with than the others. Enter your bonus points below.

Then add your *survey points* with your bonus points to get your *total points.*

SURVEY POINTS __________

+

BONUS POINTS __________

=

TOTAL POINTS __________

There are 420 possible *survey points* and 80 possible *bonus points* for a total of 500 possible *total points.*

IF YOU SCORED . . .

- **450–500** total points, your life is *extraordinarily* well balanced and you have already attained an *exceptionally* high degree of intentionality in your lifestyle. Simplicity is an old, dear friend of yours. (On the other hand, you didn't fudge the truth a little on this survey, did you?)
- **400–449** total points, you are in an *enviable situation*, with a great deal that other people could learn from you. Congratulations! Has your lifestyle always been this healthy or have you had to work on it?
- **350–399** total points, you have *good strengths in most areas* of the survey. You are likely to enjoy most aspects of your life and probably have people who look up to you because of some of the choices you've made in living an integrated life.
- **300–349** total points, you have *many things in order* in your life and are likely to be quite content. You might benefit by looking back over the survey to see if there is a particular area or two in which you need more help.
- **250–299** total points, you have *much of the raw stuff* needed to forge a simpler lifestyle, but you could benefit from some significant changes in the not-too-distant future. You have

enough that is healthy in your life so you may find that changes come fairly easily, once you commit to them.

- **200–249** total points, you are longing for quite a number of significant changes in your lifestyle fairly soon because there are just too many things that don't seem to be working well. This is not all that surprising. After all, if you weren't struggling in the first place, you probably wouldn't have picked up this book and taken this survey. You may want to seek out a friend or counselor in whom to confide your longings.
- **100–200** total points, you probably require immediate, substantial changes in your lifestyle in most areas. A good counselor would be able to help you think through your reasonable options and work with you on the skills necessary to attain them. You're longing for change in enough areas that once you get going with your lifestyle overhaul, you may find that you make very good progress in a short period of time.
- **0–99** total points, you are likely *very* unhappy and could benefit from some significant counseling. Remember: Hurting, distress, anxiety, depression, and intense longings may well be the Holy Spirit's way of signaling us that we need to make some changes in our lives. We wrote this book especially for you, friend. We pray that God works a little miracle in your life. Read on. . . .

The lifestyle survey above is a map or indicator of the paths you have chosen in some key areas of your life. Some of those paths have been well-chosen habits that conform to God's creative will. May God bless and increase the value of these paths. Others merely conform to what other people expect of you, whether they are for your good or not. These latter paths were not blazed by Christ but by the hacking and chopping of a society that puts self first, at the expense of others, and especially at the expense of a healthy relationship with God. You can identify these murky ruts because they take energy *from* your relationship with God, and they take energy *from* your love for others. Perhaps the results of the survey can help you to name some of the areas in which you are likely to stray from the more helpful paths.

Don't be surprised that you have made some bad choices in how you live your life. The ruts of needless complexity, messed-up values, and burnout into which you have walked have been trodden by many people before you. It is the better part of wisdom to admit where your lifestyle is not as it should be and to press on toward health.

But let's be clear about the true goal. As you proceed through this book, in a process that has every possibility of bringing greater simplicity into your life, don't seek simplicity, *seek God*! God alone is able to effect the changes you desire.

Søren Kierkegaard wrote *Purity of Heart Is to Will One Thing* in 1847. His grounding for this call to focus on the one thing that is truly important—God—is from James 4:8: " 'Draw nigh to God and he will draw nigh to you. Cleanse your hands, ye sinners; and purify your hearts, ye double-minded.' For only the pure in heart can see God, and therefore draw nigh to Him; and only by God drawing nigh to them can they maintain this purity. And he who in truth wills only one thing can will only the Good . . ." (*A Kierkegaard Anthology*, edited by Robert Bretall, p. 271).

Are you uncertain of your ability to seek God's simplicity with sincerity? Do you lack the kind of pure heart that seeks to draw near to God? You do well to be honest enough to admit that you are oftentimes double-minded, even on important issues. But don't give up. *Pray* for that heart to be given to you. "Ask and it will be given to you . . ." (Matt. 7:7, NIV). If you truly are being called to a deeper, more integrated walk with your Lord, the urge toward health will not soon go away. The gift of simplicity has been given to you, and you will not be satisfied until you open and use that gift.

Seek *simplicity* and you will fail; seek *God* and you will find what you truly seek.

## CHAPTER 3

# Keeping a Personal Journal

*"My heart is stirred by a noble theme*
*as I recite my verses for the king;*
*my tongue is the pen of a skillful writer."*
PSALM 45:1 (NIV)

If you are troubled enough or care enough about aspects of your present lifestyle to be reading this book, perhaps you are being called by God to make some changes in your life along the road to simplicity. If so, it may be safe to assume that you also have been called (1) to reflect on your life and (2) to listen to what God has to say to you about it.

One of the very best helps in this process of reflecting and listening is keeping a personal journal. Then, when your heart is "stirred by a noble theme," as the psalmist wrote in Psalm 45:1, you have a regular way of expressing your insights into yourself and into God's own heart.

Without the practice of keeping a journal, many valuable thoughts and insights slide into our lives and bring a momentary appreciation on our part. But then the memory of these gems dissipates into our busyness and may or may not surface again.

### Why keep a regular personal journal?

At times, our own entries into a personal journal express something we have felt but have never put into words. As such, the insight may have been a heartfelt truth at some deep level but still not have been of *conscious* use to us. In other words, you may believe something to be true but still not *know* that you believe it. Or you may not have *confidence* in your belief. That renders the belief far less useful to you. Hence, you may find yourself writing a thought in your personal journal, stop, and exclaim, "That's right! I really do believe that. Isn't that interesting." Then, because you took time to record that insight, you will be able to draw on it and dwell on it and grow from it for years to come.

David shares examples from his own journal writing:

*We keep a journal of insights for each of our kids that we plan to give them one day. Usually, they are observations about them as they mature. But sometimes we write things from our own hearts that we want them to learn. Some years ago, I wrote something for my daughter, Kate, who was four at the time. I remember sensing that my upcoming overseas trip was potentially dangerous. I could be involved in a plane crash. Someone could knock me off to steal the $30,000 worth of television equipment with which I would be traveling. Who knows what else could happen? I wanted to leave a message for my young daughter, to say that it was all right to go on this trip even if it turned out bad for me.*

> *January 27, 1987*
> *. . . Next month I go to Tanzania to produce and direct a TV documentary for Operation Bootstrap Africa. They build schools in Africa. I'll be careful so I come back safely, but remember that at times we must take reasonable risks to stand for things that matter. . . . Work for things you believe in. . . . It can be exciting to serve God! . . .*
> *Love,*
> *Your Daddy*

*I have thought hundreds of times since then about what came from my own pen: ". . . at times we must take reasonable risks to stand for things that matter. . . ." As a result of writing those words, I am certain I have subsequently done more of it. It's not that I had never stood for anything previously. But until I had written those words and reflected on them, I don't think I knew that taking "reasonable risks to stand for things that matter" was a key element of my personality and something I wanted to do more of in the future.*

*You can see that journaling is not a passive method of recording what happened, facts; it is a dynamic practice that has the power to make an imprint on your own future and that of others if you so desire.*

*It is important to review one's journal entries from time to time. The years can bring a perspective on your entries that ripen and bear fruit later. I don't always do so. I wish I had not lost track of the wisdom expressed in the following journal entry:*

> *2/3/79*
> *The kind of burning in the heart that I need in life comes from excitement . . . of a depth like that of the two men going to Emmaus [Luke 24:13-35]. I need life to be an adventure. But that doesn't come from living hard and trying too hard. It comes first from living the life of peace. . . .*

*It boggles my mind to wonder how my life would have been different had I bothered to read these words—my own words!—during the following decade, when I was living hard and trying too hard to prove myself. Only in recent years have I found peace a worthy base from which to experience an inner "Emmaus" kind of excitement (Luke 24:13-35).*

*Journaling also is a terrific time to speculate on the hazards that lie just ahead, and in that to be reminded of the source of one's strengths. Before writing the books, the articles, the devotionals, and the video scripts of recent years, I had already identified one of the potential pitfalls of writing:*

> *12/25/81*
> *Strengthen me, Lord. Be with me.*
> *If you don't live through my writing,*
> *then it will be too lonely a process*
> *for me to endure.*
> *I write for you as I live for you—*
> *in gratitude—with ultimate confidence.*
> *Amen.*

*Does keeping a journal mean always having to express confident answers to life's struggles and questions? Of course not. It may, in fact, raise questions that require years of deliberation and action.*

*I remember knowing during my senior year of seminary that some of the deepest and most enduring traits I needed for ministry were still being formed in me. It bothered me that I didn't have it all pulled together before heading out, later that year, to my first parish. So I recorded these few thoughts:*

> *1/16/82*
> *What must I do to have a steadiness of faith, stalwart obedience, and persistent habits? I honestly don't know. More on this later.*

*No answers there. But there's a pretty good question. I had taken time to express my longings for these gifts of the Spirit. Have I acquired steadiness of faith, stalwart obedience (that sounds painful), and persistent habits over the ensuing years of ordained ministry? Another good question. More on this later.*

Good questions and honest reflection in a personal journal ultimately drive the writer to God. Morton Kelsey helps us avoid the trap of feeling that our journaling is strictly for *self*-improvement or *self*-preoccupation. He wrote in *Adventure Inward*, ". . . the goal of keeping the record of my life and struggle is not so much to forge the chain of growth as to bring my inner being to the blacksmith" (Kelsey, *Adventure Inward*, p. 28).

## How to keep a regular personal journal

We will offer here just enough guidance on keeping a personal journal that you can get a *start* if you have never worked with one before. If a journal seems to work especially well for you, you will want to read a book or two devoted solely to this fascinating subject. Please note in the Annotated Bibliography a list of books we recommend on the subject.

For now, here are some of the nuts and bolts you will need to fulfill the journaling assignments we recommend in our six-week journey toward a simpler life:

- If possible, buy a bound, blank book or sketchbook at a bookstore, office supply store, or art store to use as your journal. Notebooks, notes, and loose pages are too casual for your insights and will not last through the years of further review and reflection. For the same reason, consider using a pen rather than a pencil. You're writing for the ink to endure, not to be published or even to have anyone else read. Yes, you *could* use a typewriter or computer. Yes, we know you can express yourself faster that way. But isn't the goal to think *deeply* rather than to write quickly? Trust us; write longhand.

- Keep the journal in a private place where people aren't likely to happen upon it. You don't want to tempt them to snoop, nor edit your entries out of fear that others will read them. Be sure to put a request on your title page for the casual person to respect the privacy of the journal and put it down immediately.
- You won't have to cross out or correct many "mistakes" of spelling, grammar, or details since the goal is honest and free expression, not accuracy of jots and tittles.
- Begin each entry by noting the date in the journal. Occasionally, you will want to add to that a brief description of the circumstances under which you write your entry (for example, "Written the day I got the new job" or "Deeply discouraged today"). This will help you find what you seek when you scan for that entry later.
- Make your journal entries on a *regular* basis. Daily is best because it's a habit that's easy to neglect. But if you are the kind of person who is likely to sabotage your own best intentions for developing a new daily habit—there are a bunch of us out there—then keep coming back to your journal whenever you have sufficient grace to do so. And don't chastise yourself for the days/months/years you missed. Just rejoice that you have been called to write another day.
- Are you a morning person or an evening person? Make journal entries at a time when you are more likely to be alert (not tired) and reflective. A lit candle can help you to focus and give the time a set-apart-for-something-special kind of feeling.
- Share your journal entries *sparingly*, if at all, with others. Very few people have the wisdom, perspective, and experience to give you helpful feedback on what you have written. A spiritual guide or director will have such training; a pastor might; others, probably not. Resist the temptation to show and tell. Let your journaling be between you and your Lord, for the most part.

- Feel free to record your own struggles and insights as well as how you sense God responding to you.
- Pick the journal up now and then just to read previous entries. Your life will have a deeper and more intentional perspective because of it. Do this especially if you have fallen out of the practice; you will be reminded of why this is such a splendid tool for spiritual growth and you will be motivated to begin again.
- Keep a regular personal journal that fits *you*. By all means, write as the *Spirit* leads, not necessarily as this book or any other suggests. Use only what seems to be of value in this chapter and discard the rest.

## A very special method of journaling

David shares:

*Allow me to finish this chapter by sharing with you a very special method of journaling that has been a particular blessing to me in recent years. If it is of value to even a few readers it will be worth sharing.*

*One day, I pulled from my bookshelves a small volume,* A Thousand Reasons for Living, *by Dom Helder Camara (Fortress, 1981). I paged through and quickly found a few delightful "meditations" that had caught my fancy. Like. . . .*

*A warning to the prosperous*

*It is not easy*
*to preserve*
*the soul of a jeep*
*in a Cadillac body.*

*2 January 1962*

*and*

*Do people weigh you down?*

*Don't carry them on your shoulders.*
*Take them into your heart.*

*30 August 1962*

*Poetry without rhyme. Wisdom without pretense. Just pithy, inspired insights. I loved it. I was moved to write as directly as possible—in a similar style—what God showed me in my devotional time. Having spent the summer of 1980 house-sitting for Elizabeth Qualley, the sister and only sibling of the late American poet e. e. cummings (who used only lowercase letters in his writing), I decided that when the voice in the writing was my own, I would use only such letters and no punctuation as a symbolic way of showing deference to God. And when the voice was God speaking to me, I would use normal punctuation and both upper- and lower-case letters.*

*The first day, my journal entry included this description of the excitement I felt during my devotional time with God:*

*12 December 1990*

**lifting**
*i lift a flap of eternity and i peek*
*looking for you*
*i am a boy*
*stealing a glimpse of the circus*
*through a vent in the fabric*
*of your tent*
*i am transfixed*

*At times, the voice of God in my regular devotional time seemed to be saying something specific enough for me to record and remember. Here is an example from the first day this happened to me. It doesn't take a Freudian psychoanalyst to figure out that this was written during a time when I was feeling an acute longing for a simpler life. Note that the use of uppercase letters indicates that this is God talking to me:*

*13 December 1990*

**Demands**
*With chin on your chest*
*you furrow your brow*
*and shovel demands all day.*
*Joy is a memory*
*love is a luxury*

*intensity is here to stay—*
*or so you say.*
*Here—*
*put down the shovel*
*let me rub your brow,*
*and while you're resting*
*I'll straighten a few things for you.*
*There—*
*Better?*
*You just had a little inflammation*
*of the demand gland.*
*The shovel?*
*Funny, it was here a moment ago. . . .*

*The ending surprised even me and gave me a chuckle. I left my devotional time feeling lighter, minus the "shovel" I often wield to deal with an overabundance of demands I often allow to accumulate. Journaling doesn't always have to be an intense, serious time. Often it is freeing, relaxing, and full of grace.*

Enjoy your time of guided journaling during the six weeks of exploring simplicity that we offer in Chapters 4–9 of this book. Could you get away with skipping the journaling part of the six-week process? Certainly. But if you avoid the temptation to take that shortcut, a deeper, more enjoyable, more direct link with God is what awaits you on the journey.

*Bon voyage!*

# CHAPTER 4

# WEEK ONE—Getting a Quick Start

Congratulations.

You've gotten past the point of casual interest you might initially have had in browsing through this book. You have now come to the section of the book where you will begin the intentional process of moving toward a simpler life.

## Six-Week Format

In the next six weeks you will combine your good intentions for a simpler, more integrated life with (1) Bible readings, (2) action ideas, (3) times of reflection, primarily through journaling, and (4) pithy quotes and insights from others who have journeyed before you.

We generally will be using an Action/Reflection model of lifestyle change where the goal is to act on our longings, then reflect on them and make appropriate modifications to our actions. An action model without reflection would offer little or no understanding and the action wouldn't last. Occasionally the process will be a Reflection/Action model, though its problem is that one can fail to get beyond the good intentions and it remains only reflection, with few or no positive results.

## The Quick Start

Your goal is a simpler life. To that end, our goal in the beginning is to get you off to a quick start. According to *Consumer Reports* (December 1993 issue), WeightWatchers, the highly rated weight loss program, stresses that *long-term*, balanced weight loss is the goal. But it also takes into account that people need early successes to reward their initial good intentions.

We believe the need for early successes is important to any substantive and enduring program of changes we attempt. So get ready to see a difference in your life this first week. We hope to provide you with some of the raw stuff that will usher you into some early successes in living a simpler, more integrated life, as well as some elements of long-term balance that will last a lifetime.

In upcoming days and weeks, we will ask you to reflect on what is happening in your life, providing insights that will lead you to continue in a certain direction or make appropriate changes in course. This process of reflection, primarily through your journaling, *should not be undermined.* Literally. There is rich "mining" to do in the vein of the wisdom that God's own Spirit gives to you. If you bypass the reflection process, you may have a short jaunt into some changes, but you won't value them properly and you won't know—really know—why those changes work for you. If so, the benefits may be short-lived. If you want only temporary relief from a lifestyle that leaves you overwhelmed and overextended, the action ideas might be enough. But *if you are looking for the long-term good, please don't take shortcuts.* Reflection is a critical part of the long-term good.

In our research, we discovered that it takes about six weeks for a new habit to become the norm in a person's life. Those who want and need changes in their lives badly enough will let time work in their favor. Weeks of effective action and reflection will translate into enduring relief and healthy new directions.

God bless you now on your journey.

## DAY ONE—There Are Reasons

*"God whispers in our pleasures but shouts in our pain."*
C. S. Lewis

There are reasons why you may be weary of the way your life has been going. There are reasons why you may be hurting.

There are reasons why you are longing for changes in your lifestyle.

We have discovered that the discomfort that led us into a simpler life was, in fact, a gift from God. If we had not felt the discomfort that was a natural and expected result of the poor choices we had made, we would not have longed for the changes that have been such a blessing to us.

A person usually would not thank God for the searing pain that comes after putting a hand on the hot burner of a stove. And yet if that pain were not present, the person would continue leaning on the burner until irreparable damage has occurred. Pain is a gift! That pain is like the voice of a loving parent saying, "Be careful, dear one, I don't want you to get damaged by what you are doing. I love you too much to let that happen."

Isn't it possible that the very discomfort that has caused you to seek a simpler life is a gift from God? If you were to continue in some of the hurtful directions your life has taken, just *imagine* the lasting damage that could occur!

**SCRIPTURE:** Romans 5:1-5

> *Therefore, since we have been justified through faith, we have peace with God through our Lord Jesus Christ.*
>
> ROM. 5:1 (NIV)

**ACTION IDEA:**

Make a list of the three most pressing changes you need to make in your lifestyle. (You will be tipped off to the need to change by the degree of pain, anxiety, or anguish that false priorities have caused you. Check the lifestyle survey and notice items with low numbers.) Choose one of those three desired changes and plan something concrete you can do to affect that one area for the better in the next twenty-four hours (for example, not stay late at work, start exercising, do something fun with your family or friends). This is a modest goal but an important one. God certainly forgives us when we fail, but God also calls us to renewal (see Rom. 12:1-2).

**JOURNALING:**

Where does it hurt? Your inner pain and suffering very likely are good indicators of the need for change in your life. For

*one noisy world back into another. Small hands or big, we must learn to recognize the signs that our inner life is on overload. Slow those thoughts. Create positive self-talk. Don't feel you must always pass sentence on yourself, making critical comments that others never hear aloud. Learn to hear the quiet voice once again.*

**SCRIPTURE:** Psalm 46:10, 1 Kings 19:11-12

*Be still, and know that I am God;*
*I will be exalted among the nations,*
*I will be exalted in the earth.* PSALM 46:10 (NIV)

**ACTION IDEA:**

Today, choose one image or phrase to take with you into the day. Use the calming words of Psalm 46:10 if you like. Or use the "Jesus Prayer," the subject of an anonymous classic Christian book, *The Way of a Pilgrim*. The prayer is simple: "Jesus Christ, Son of God, have mercy on me, a sinner." Whenever your thoughts become jumbled or noisy, bring those words or a helpful picture to mind until you feel peaceful again. Finding focus through a phrase or a visual image in your mind's eye is an effective way of importing a sense of focus to other areas of your life.

**JOURNALING:**

Write about your chosen words or image. Why did you choose that particular phrase or picture? Concentrate on your phrase or symbol for a minute or two and see how it develops. Does the scene enlarge? Do people enter? Do the words bring forth other words? Let your thoughts grow but bring them back to the single image or phrase before you write.

You have completed week two on your six-week journey. Hopefully, week one got you off to a good start and week two built on that beginning by helping you to listen to your longings, to reevaluate your time commitments, to slow down, to sense your calling into a simpler lifestyle, to recognize your brokenness and God's power to heal, to cease some destructive habits, and to carve out some time for personal retreat. Make a special week-end journal entry, observing how your listening skills are improving. In particular, how is your journaling time helping you to be more attentive to the process in your heart and mind?

CHAPTER 6

# WEEK THREE—
# Naming the Struggles

## DAY ONE—Pruning

*"Although today He prunes*
*my twigs with pain,*
*Yet doth His blood nourish*
*and warm my root;*
*Tomorrow I shall put forth*
*buds once again*
*And clothe myself with*
*fruit."* Christina Rossetti, from *House to House*

Barbara shares:

*We had moved into a house that had been empty and neglected for some time. The most obvious flaw was the landscaping. Shrubs had grown into trees. Overgrown branches crawled across the borders that divided grass from stone. Worms had invaded the birch trees and nibbled small holes in the leaves. Armed with a pair of clippers and no experience, I began to chop away at the jungled mess. Worms fell into my hair. Scratches appeared on my bare arms and legs. Soon a pile of defeated branches lay at my feet. The tree looked better but the shrubs underneath reminded me of one of those pixie haircuts you get when you're little and it's hot and nobody wants to mess with long hair.*

*Six inches from the ground a few scraggly, bare branches stuck out of the rocks. I thought I had killed them. They grew back. Beautiful, full and round. I thought it a miracle. Most people know it's just the way nature works. What they don't always know is that it can work for human nature, too.*

*Pruning. It doesn't sound pleasant. But all good gardeners do it. That's if they want things to turn out right in the end. It produces a miracle or two. Fruits of the Spirit hanging heavy on the tree.*

*If it's a simpler life you desire, prepare to be pruned. It's a messy job but somebody has to do it. Get rid of the worms. Cut back the overgrowth. Take it right down to the root. It requires some patience. You may not like what you see when you get done. But in time . . . in time.*

**SCRIPTURE:** John 15:1-11

> *"I am the true vine, and my Father is the gardener. He cuts off every branch in me that bears no fruit, while every branch that does bear fruit he prunes so that it will be even more fruitful."* **JOHN 15:1-2 (NIV)**

**ACTION IDEA:**

In what areas of your life are you overextended or overwhelmed? Where could you prune back your schedule to allow time for new growth? If possible, make a commitment to keep evening meetings to two or less a week. Look at your calendar. Which activities could be dropped? You may need to work on this "cutting back" little by little, but stick to it. Maybe your stepping back will allow another possibility to come forward. Block off time on your calendar for your important relationships. When people ask you to schedule them into those reserved slots, just tell them you are busy. No need to explain that it is with family or friends. Treat your key relationships as at least as important as your business or volunteer commitments.

**JOURNALING:**

When you made some choices in the action idea above, you reprioritized one thing over another. You made an active decision to treat a neglected area with the importance it deserves. Why did you choose what you chose? How does it feel to have that area in your life restored to its rightful place?

## DAY TWO—Let's Name It

> *"It is by those who have suffered that the world has been advanced."* Tolstoy

We all carry unfinished business around with us. Part of a simpler life is learning to deal with the unfinished business.

The relationships that have been put on hold. The temper that always gets the best of you. That secret desire to one-up if given the chance. You name it. In fact, you are the only person who can name it. Giving our brokenness a name is the first step toward reconciling that part of our personalities that we haven't given back to God.

We attended a family camp one summer in which large numbers of mentally challenged adults were included. At first, some of the other children were scared. These new friends acted differently and some had physical handicaps as well. But, as the week went on, it was obvious who had the greater capacity to love. After a couple of days the differences that made us all a little awkward seemed to take the back seat. Our new friends wore their brokenness on the outside. We wore ours on the inside. I was glad mine was where it didn't show as much. If I had to wear my brokenness—my unfinished business—where it showed, I wondered what I would look like. We all, because of our human condition, are somewhat disabled and disfigured.

When looking for role models of the simpler life, where should we look? Look first to those who have suffered—the ones who live in "the great tribulation." It will do two things. It will allow you to see yourself and your problems in perspective and it will challenge you to suffer a little yourself. Not that we need any martyrs on this journey. North American "suffering" can't hold a candle to the rest of the world. Ours usually is an inner pain, the kind that comes when we realize how far off the track we've gone, the kind that comes when we look at all we've accumulated and say, "Is that all there is?" That's First-World suffering. Mother Teresa calls it "spiritual poverty." That's a twist. The poor feeling sorry for us. What do they know that we don't know?

**SCRIPTURE:** Hebrews 11:32-40, Revelation 7:9-14

*After this I looked and there before me was a great multitude that no one could count, from every nation, tribe, people and language, standing before the throne and in front of the Lamb. They were wearing white robes and were holding palm branches in their hands.* REV. 7:9 (NIV)

**ACTION IDEA:**

How distant have you kept yourself from people who are unlike yourself? How far away from your neighborhood is the other side of the tracks? Find a safe way to take a drive through or volunteer in an area where you usually wouldn't put yourself. Go with a group to a homeless shelter, food kitchen, or safe house. See how others live and then listen to the pain.

**JOURNALING:**

Reflect on the haves and the have-nots. As you watch the nightly news, how is your life different from what you see on the screen? What advantages/disadvantages have you been given? How would someone from a Third-World country respond to the life you have created for yourself? Why is it important to get some perspective on how many material things we have compared to the rest of the world, and where we may be "poor"?

## DAY THREE—Lion Taming

*"In times when the government imprisons any unjustly, the true place for a just man is also the prison."*

Henry David Thoreau

In *Living Simply Through the Day*, Tilden Edwards describes a dream that was told to him by a friend. The friend saw Jesus sitting on a rock, quietly in prayer. The friend also sat, but not so quietly. He felt restless and struggled to settle himself. Frustrated, he stood to go, only to see that Jesus had become restless and agitated. The man returned and sat down to find that as Jesus struggled, the man's own soul had become more peaceful.

"Doing justice" means to take on the agitations and restlessness of another. It means we confront the lions. If we are "to do justice" we must go to where those who are treated unfairly dwell—where the lions roar the loudest. Sometimes the journey takes us into other continents. Sometimes we need only look across the dinner table, at family members or friends. Sometimes the journey takes us into our own hearts.

Edwards calls this journey of justice the "complementarity of life," ". . . suffering for another so s/he can be free of suffering, of giving so another can receive, of receiving as another gives." This necessary call to justice gives a natural order to things. When we mess with this order—ignoring the need to work for justice on behalf of others—we help to create a world out of balance. This, in turn, creates a breeding ground for all types of further brokenness.

The concept of equality or justice becomes a real possibility when people view themselves as only part of a larger whole, not self-sufficient but in need of the gifts of others as they are in need of our gifts. Why is it so difficult to express needs and weaknesses in ourselves? Maybe the injustice that needs correcting dwells under our own roof. We do not always need to be the fixers. Sometimes we are the ones who need fixing. In truth, we are both—fixer and the one broken, healer but also wounded.

"When we ignore the truth of complementarity, and treat ourselves as a central empire to be served, and turn man and nature over to this exclusive self-service, then a cry of agony resounds in heaven. Freedom is misspent. Great suffering ensues. A web of distorted acts builds networks of vanity, violence and delusion. . ." (Edwards, p. 160). The lions roar then. Mouths open. Teeth sharpened, looking for meat.

The lesson is simple. Part but not all. Some but not everything. Restraint and not indulgence. Giving and receiving. Freedom for the imprisoned may mean imprisonment for the free. Suffering so another can be free of suffering. These feed the hungry lions, and they are nothing that Christ hasn't already done for us.

**SCRIPTURE:** Micah 6:8

*He has showed you, O man, what is good.*
*And what does the LORD require of you?*
*To act justly and to love mercy*
*and to walk humbly with your God.*

MICAH 6:8 (NIV)

**ACTION IDEA:**

Today, search the daily newspaper. Look for stories where injustice has been done. If possible, choose to "do justice" on one of those issues. Write a letter to your member of Congress of other governmental decision makers, or a letter to the editor of your local newspaper. Send a donation or letter of support to someone who is doing a good job of trying to right a wrong.

**JOURNALING:**

Go back to the newspaper and reflect on the reasons behind the injustice. Does the suffering come from a demand of a self to be served? Where has the "complementarity of life" broken down? Write about your own perceptions and what catches your interest when you read or hear about people who are hurting. Follow your heart. Where might God be leading you?

## DAY FOUR—Motivations

> *"The world asks, 'How much does he give?' Christ asks, 'Why does he give?'"* John Raleigh Mott

It is best not to question our motivations too closely. A small glimpse now and then. A momentary wandering into self-inspection. But that's all. It's best just to get on with things. Listen to the call, try and follow and know that because you are human you never will be entirely pure in your motives. There always will exist some small piece of pride. A bit of arrogance. An undigested piece of piety. A third eye watching to see how others react. Lord, help us.

The yearning for a simpler life and clearer priorities comes from God. So does the ability to act on that desire. It takes the pressure off. Our only bit in the whole process is to keep our senses open for the call when it comes and not turn away from where we are being led. Some call that being blind. Some call it being obedient. It's good to remember that Jesus healed a blind man, but only after the man allowed Jesus to place a mixture of mud and spit on his eyes could he see (John 9:6-7).

Mud and spit are good images for a call into simplicity. There's nothing too arrogant about saliva, nothing pious about dirt. They are common elements, much like bread and wine. Food for the blind.

There is a lesson in all of this. Look at the tools by which Jesus did his work. Twelve rather common men of that time: fisherman, businessmen, and a tax collector. Women with somewhat questionable reputations. Three siblings: Mary, Martha, and Lazarus. Water into wine, fish that fed thousands, a calmed wind. Finally, a wooden cross and some nails. There's nothing flashy here, although the ending wasn't bad. Nothing to make us think that he ever worried about arrogance or a prideful nature. He was too intent on listening.

Again and again he coaxed us to follow his example. "Unless you become as a little child. . . ." "Blessed are the pure in heart."

Why have we hung heavy theologies on such a simple man? When he wore a common robe and a pair of sandals, why do we mentally dress him in vestments and finery? When he chose to be born in a cave, why do we worship him in expensive buildings while tossing a "benevolent" sum to those who sleep on streets and on top of heating vents? It was not his way. What have we done? Why have we done it? Perhaps this is the time to question our motivation.

A call into simplicity is a call back to the basics, a committed choice not only to worship God but to follow the teachings. And don't worry about your motivations. You're hanging on to the hem of his garment now. It's a safe place from which to do your business.

**SCRIPTURE:** Matthew 9:20-22, 15:7-9

*Jesus turned and saw her. "Take heart, daughter," he said, "your faith has healed you." And the woman was healed from that moment.* MATT. 9:22 (NIV)

**ACTION IDEA:**

Get back to the basics and make some space to do some mending or fixing today. Shorten that skirt or fix that shelf—they have been waiting there for awhile. If nothing else, find a little one who is ready to learn how to hem or hammer and observe while he or she practices. All the while, think about the woman in today's Scripture and the space Jesus made for her, even in the midst of his great busy-ness.

**JOURNALING:**

Take on the role of the woman in today's Scripture. Or try on the voice of Jesus as he talked with her. What did she say? How did Jesus respond to her? Record your dialogue in your journal entry for today. How do you feel when you approach God? Do you expect to be noticed or heard? What are your motivations for seeking God? What are God's motivations for seeking us?

## DAY FIVE—Blind Ponies

> *"But the boys never did saddle or bridle it. They knew how dangerous it was to ride a blind pony."* Jim Heynen

In Jim Heynen's story "The Blind Pony," two boys make endless attempts to harness a pony blind in one eye from birth. But what the pony didn't have in sight, he more than made up for in hearing. The one good eye and two good ears compensated for the loss of vision. The boys' attempts failed over and over. Finally, the boys tried an apple. The pony's nose was as good as his ears. The pony would come at the sound of the boys climbing the apple tree and sniff out the inviting fruit. "Why didn't we think of this before?" the boys lamented.

Great pride can be taken in taming an animal or an undisciplined spirit, for that matter. Sometimes the most obvious answers come only after countless attempts at something that seemed like a good idea at the time but led back to the same old problem.

Society has been working hard to solve all the problems that have been caused by our own seeming success. Stress symptoms, time crunches, a general malaise that settles over any society that has fed itself a false bill of goods. The climb up isn't nearly as painful as the climb down.

Longing for simplicity can be like chasing a blind pony. Sometimes the answer seems evasive, almost impossible. It's easier to study simplicity than to engage it. Keep feeding it with a good book or a motivated speaker. Perhaps even contemplate the food chain or the effect of a throwaway society. The day needs to come when we put down the book, set down the contemplating, saddle that pony, and ride it. It's better to be bucked off, to remount and ride again than never to have ridden at all.

**SCRIPTURE:** Hebrews 12:1-2

> *Therefore, since we are surrounded by such a great cloud of witnesses, let us throw off everything that hinders and the sin that so easily entangles, and let us run with perseverance the*

*race marked out for us. Let us fix our eyes on Jesus, the author and perfecter of our faith, who for the joy set before him endured the cross, scorning its shame, and sat down at the right hand of the throne of God.* HEB. 12:1-2 (NIV)

**ACTION IDEA:**

As you have been reading these action ideas, you even may have stopped for a moment and said, "That's a good idea!" But have you acted? Have you found a way to tame the pony? Glance back over the ideas that have been presented to you but which you might have put off for one reason or another. Take another took at the lifestyle survey. How are you doing in terms of time, family and friends, finances, or physical, emotional, or spiritual health? Choose an area and plan one action that is workable for you today. Do it.

**JOURNALING:**

You may have heard the call. You may be longing for simplicity. Yet in some ways it evades you. Reflect on what may be stopping you from acting on your good intentions. You may need to do some confessing to break through this barrier. You may need to talk with others. Continue to ask God for help and guidance.

## DAY SIX—Have You Laughed Today?

*"It only hurts when I laugh."* Universal

In our first book on this topic, *'Tis a Gift to Be Simple*, we told the story of a sincere Christian man who helped spearhead the idea of wiping out hunger in Haiti. If you know anything about Haiti and the political unrest that has damaged that country, you know that what he and others proposed to do was, in this world, impossible. They have, however, over the last few years, made a significant improvement in the lives of some Haitians, most of them students of a Haitian Christian school, who are served better meals than they normally would receive and whose educations are guaranteed. Their intent is serious. The Haitians' condition is serious. But at the fund-raisers you should hear this man and his friends laugh while they're having fun.

He is not the first to use laughter to ease pain. And I have no doubt that he is still at his "serious" business because he has learned to laugh. Burned-out people aren't known for their infectious laughter.

With this in mind, our "quote of the day" may be somewhat flawed. One rewording could be "I only laugh when it hurts." This is not to say that we ignore our pain or cover it with false hilarity. It is to say that people who take themselves too seriously will not last. Simplicity, played out in the life of someone who cannot enjoy its fruits, will shrivel into cynicism and contempt. If we listen to the pain, in ourselves and in others, if we allow the time for some introspection, if we do not always like what we find there, we will need some tolerance of ourselves. Golda Meir once said, "Don't be humble. You're not that great." We are, in all our confusions, comical and not to be taken too seriously.

Suffering is not funny. Dealing with the consequences of our sin is not funny. A world where some people live in excess while others don't have enough to survive is not funny. It is a sad and broken world. It is also God's world and "I will rejoice in it!" What other choice do I have that allows me to continue?

**SCRIPTURE:** Psalm 98:6-9, 126:1-3

> *Our mouths were filled with laughter,*
> *our tongues with songs of joy.*
> *Then it was said among the nations,*
> *"The LORD has done great things for them."*
>
> PS. 126:2 (NIV)

**ACTION IDEA:**

Rent a *Three Stooges* movie or play a laugh track. Read something hilarious and let yourself enjoy it. Take a laughing break.

**JOURNALING:**

Record all the things that make you chuckle. Try and include as many of these "stress relievers" in your day as you can. Recall the times you laughed today, last week, and at various times in the past. What was it that brought you pleasure? Try to experience it again.

## DAY SEVEN—Saying Good-bye

*"Every parting gives a foretaste of death; every coming together again a foretaste of the Resurrection."*

Arthur Schopenhauer

Our boy, Reed, just turned six. He's a good boy with a kind heart. He still can think himself into tears with only a sad memory, although he tries harder now to hold it together. Saying "good-bye" just about does him in. Leaving a grandparent's home still tears him up. Sometimes we worry about him. He cares so deeply. Other times we just feel proud that he can love like that.

Saying good-bye to people, places, or even things can be a sad experience. We've all felt that tug to stay pulling against the tug to get in the car and be on our way. We don't always wear our struggle on our faces like Reed. But it tears us up somewhere.

In looking for a simpler life, we are looking, in fact, to make a change—in some ways to say "good-bye" to some aspects of our life. It is a death in part. More like a divorce, really. For those who have experienced it, some say a divorce is harder because the person is still around but the relationship is dead. It's over, but not really.

You may have sensed already that a call for simplicity includes the word "good-bye." Good-bye to a certain lifestyle, even if it caused you pain. Good-bye to some friends because they may not want to go with you on this new journey. Good-bye to blind consumption because it feels good. Good-bye to an apathetic approach to the world's ills.

But you know the resurrection story: To every parting there is a coming together and to every death a promised new life.

In the musical *Oklahoma*, Will Parker, having met his competition in a salesman who gives "Persian good-byes," introduces his Ado Annie to an "Oklahoma hello." It does the trick; she's smitten and off they go together.

This book is like an "Oklahoma hello." Our competition is tough. It's a flashy world out there. Egos are on the line. Change doesn't always come easy. But if Will Parker can win the affections of Ado Annie with a good kiss, Jesus should have no problem winning our attention by laying down his life. It's a matter of trust, and sometimes you just have to jump.

**SCRIPTURE:** 1 Samuel 20:41-42

*Jonathon said to David, "Go in peace, for we have sworn friendship with each other in the name of the LORD, saying, 'The LORD is witness between you and me, and between your descendants and my descendants forever.' " Then David left, and Jonathon went back to the town.*

**1 SAM. 20:42 (NIV)**

**ACTION IDEA:**

You are now at the midway point in your six-week journey toward a simpler lifestyle. You have dealt this week with struggles in your actions and motivations, with time commitments, reaching out to others, facing injustice, taming your "ponies," and laughing. If you take time to review the week, you will see that you have some tools that are needed, especially in this in-between time, when you may be tempted to quit this journey toward a simpler lifestyle.

You've learned to say "good-bye" to some things but to laugh because of the freedom your life's changes have afforded you. Time again to celebrate! Set aside some time today to celebrate fresh developments in your life by bringing some freshness into someone else's life. Bring the gift of music (sing, play an instrument, buy a compact disk, write a song) to someone you love. Enjoy the music together, then take a walk to enjoy the greater openness we hope you are feeling.

**JOURNALING:**

Write words of praise to God that reflect your highest hopes and joys. If you have not already done so, you might try to write these thoughts into a poem or as lyrics for a song. Later, find a friend who can help you craft these words into a hymn or song that can be used in church or Sunday school.

# CHAPTER 7

# WEEK FOUR—
# Serving Only God

## DAY ONE—Decluttering

> *"There is a very real sense of lightness and freedom that happens when we clean out the hall closet and throw away all the junk."*
>
> Jo Carr and Imogene Sorley, from *The Intentional Family*

Barbara shares:

*Many years back, I traveled with a choir to the Scandinavian countries. Being an inexperienced traveler, I overloaded my suitcase, picked up a couple of carry-on bags, and stashed away an empty canvas catchall in which to haul back all my purchases. Naively, I boarded the plane, expecting to enjoy myself. I did. But I learned a large lesson in the benefits of traveling light.*

*It's not a large jump to see how a popular travel tip can have something to say about simplifying one's life. Traveling light can be a metaphor for the inward journey as well as good advice for anyone traveling through life. Each decade brings more possessions, responsibilities, and memories, some of which encumber and some of which set us free.*

*I remember one winter, long past, the frustration of not being able to shut my bureau cabinet. "Too much stuff!" I muttered, pulling one sweater after another from the cramped drawers. "I need more room!" It was the first time it hit me that I really didn't need more room. I needed fewer sweaters. Sorting through the pile of "never-worn but still good" articles to give to Goodwill, I felt freed up. Wow! What a feeling! I had less trouble deciding what to wear in the morning because my choices had been limited to things I really liked. Fewer clothes meant I didn't have to fight the drawers anymore, either.*

*The same idea applies to any place that's out of control with clutter. Kitchens. Offices. Garages. What do you really need to get the job done? Keep it and share the rest. Take a look at your child's room. It's amazing that children with only a few toys can play beautifully, while an overflowing toy chest may not be enough for other children who claim to have "nothing to do."*

*"Declutter" is a popular catchword, often tied in with simplifying. It's not a bad place to start. But a word of warning. It is very contagious. Decluttering your closet leads to the other closets, into the cabinets, out into the garage, and into your very soul. Old grudges? Out they go. Harbored hurts? Who needs them. Sins of the fathers? Let them be. Take a look around. Sort through a closet or two. You'll be convinced.*

**SCRIPTURE:** Luke 6:38, 1 Corinthians 5:6-8

> *Get rid of the old yeast that you may be a new batch without yeast—as you really are. For Christ, our Passover lamb, has been sacrificed. Therefore let us keep the Festival, not with the old yeast, the yeast of malice and wickedness, but with bread without yeast, the bread of sincerity and truth.*
>
> **1 COR. 5:7-8 (NIV)**

**ACTION IDEA:**

You probably saw this one coming. Choose an area in your home that needs some attention. Haul away the excess and live with the rest. Prayer closets need attention, too. If you have a fireplace, build a fire. Write a grievance you have carried toward another person on a piece of paper. Toss the paper in the fire and let the matter go.

**JOURNALING:**

Are there thoughts and worries that keep surfacing on a daily basis that you would like to get rid of? Write them down in your journal and ask God to remove them from your mind or change them.

## DAY TWO—Try Not to Think of a Monkey

*"If a man does not keep pace with his neighbors, perhaps it is because he hears a different drummer."*

Henry David Thoreau

We play a fun mind game with our children. "Try not to think of a monkey," we say. Their answer lately is "pizza, pizza, pizza, pizza." I think they've licked that one.

When you are asked not to think of something, it seems like that's all you can think of. That's why the call to a simpler life doesn't ask you not to think of possessions or prestige. It just asks you not to worry about them. There is real freedom in giving the responsibility of ownership back to the rightful owner. A simpler life asks us to remember that the possessions we receive are not owned but borrowed. That we receive them as a gift. That we share our abundance when the real owner asks us to. The more we have the more we care for. The less we have the less we need feel responsible for. It makes sense to live with less, especially if you're feeling overextended.

When commercials bombard you with thoughts of "Try not to think of the great savings" or "Try not to think about how great that one item will look in your home," I wouldn't suggest saying "pizza" over and over. You'll probably just end up at the nearest pizza parlor, ordering a large pepperoni pizza with extra cheese.

You might try saying, "Jesus, Jesus, Jesus, Jesus" a few times. If he could calm the storms, he won't have much trouble with a few commercials.

**SCRIPTURE:** Matthew 7:24-27

*Therefore everyone who hears these words of mine and puts them into practice is like a wise man who built his house on the rock.* MATT. 7:24 (NIV)

**ACTION IDEA:**

Make a pact with yourself to buy only what you intended to buy for a whole week. Nix any impulse purchases. At the end of the week, see if you even can remember what you had wanted to add to your purchases.

**JOURNALING:**

What is the difference between a list of "wants" and a list of "needs"? What do you *really* need? What do you merely *want* that you would be willing to give up in order that others might have their *true needs* met?

## DAY THREE—The Ominous To-Do List

> *"Our whole being by its nature is one vast need; in complete, preparatory, empty yet cluttered, crying out for Him who can untie things that are now knotted together and tie up things that are still dangling loose."*
>
> C. S. Lewis, from *The Four Loves*

Barbara shares:

*My father is a great list maker. Every few days, he revises his old list of things to do into a new one. Each day is earmarked for some event or job, travel or thing to remember. It keeps him focused. It helps him get up in the morning and "get at it"!*

*There isn't a person out there who doesn't have some kind of "to-do" list going. Either in his or her head, on a piece of paper somewhere, or in his or her computer. Despite their obvious benefits, "to-do" lists can lead to two great drawbacks: You can forget to put something on the list and hence it is forgotten, or your list can become overwhelming, impossible, and lose its ability to keep you on track. Even with a list we too often can find ourselves "tied in knots" or "dangling loose."*

*I used to have the habit of making a list of things to do for the day, putting more on the list than I knew I could handle. No matter how much I accomplished during the day, no matter how much I pushed myself, I always felt that I had failed. Part of the list remained. How futile. "The list," instead of being the friend I intended, kept stabbing me in the back. I was worshiping a false god that I had created.*

*How often do you feel "tied up in knots," "dispersed," "overwhelmed," "frantic," "at wit's end"? Have you created a list that keeps you running but never lets you win? Do the words "silence," "prayer," "Bible study" appear on your list? Does your "list" keep you from spending time with family or friends?*

*Cry out for God. Ask the Spirit to edit your list, keep your priorities straight, tie up your loose ends, and untie your knots.*

**SCRIPTURE:** Luke 10:38-42

*But the LORD answered her, "Martha, Martha, you are worried and distracted by many things; there is need of only one thing. Mary has chosen the better part, which will not be taken away from her."* LUKE 10:41-42 (NIV)

**ACTION IDEA:**

Make a list (or amend your present "to do" list) to include those things that are important to you, which rarely if ever end up in writing. You might wish to check the lifestyle survey, especially the spiritual health items. Remember the theme for this week is "Serving Only God."

**JOURNALING:**

If you had a bizarre disease that allowed you to be conscious for just one hour a day, and you knew that your physical needs would be taken care of while you were unconscious, how would you use that one hour each day? Do those activities become relatively less important when you are conscious sixteen hours a day?

## DAY FOUR—Even Grace Can Be an Idol

*"Stewardship is what a man does after he says 'I believe.' "*
W. H. Greever

I (Barbara) have forgotten who was quoting whom. I only remember what the speaker said. It was a rhetorical question. "What do we do," he began, "when we don't have to do anything?" He was speaking of faith and the need to respond—do something—not because we *have* to, but because we *want* to.

At a retreat several years ago, a young man questioned some of the changes we had suggested for those wanting to try a simpler approach to their life and their possessions. "I don't need more rules in my life," he stated firmly. We tried to talk with him later, but he put us off, obviously miffed and wanting to hear more grace in our message.

I wish he would have felt comfortable enough in his disagreements to keep the dialogue open. Rules or legalism, an "I have to do this" attitude is one of the ditches a person can fall into when seeking to make some changes. We've done our fair share of that—especially in the beginning. We all need to remember that Jesus doesn't require anything of us but an open heart. And even when the line has gone dead, Jesus will hang on just in case. But it doesn't end there.

Simplicity is like a telephone call. When the phone rings, you pick it up. It's an almost automatic response to the caller. Now, I have let the phone ring on occasions when I was too busy to answer it. But that's the whole point. This is the million-dollar call. Do I really want to be so busy that I miss this one?

No, I don't have to answer the phone. I don't have to "do" anything. But, please don't go telling me that I can't, just because I don't have to. My hands are free. It's my choice to pick up the receiver, say "hello," and find out that I have an important call here.

**SCRIPTURE:** Job 34:4

*Let us discern for ourselves what is right;*
*let us learn together what is good.* JOB 34:4 (NIV)

**ACTION IDEA:**

Take a break! Do nothing today, if you want.

**JOURNALING:**

Answer the man's questions at the beginning of today's devotional. "What can I do, now that I don't *have* to do anything?" Ask yourself, "What choices do I *want* to make; what do I *want* to do?"

## DAY FIVE—The Bottom Line

*"It's not what you'd do with a million,*
*If riches should e'er be your lot,*
*But what are you doing at present*
*With the dollar and quarter you've got?"* Anonymous

It's great when things get practical. We can talk about simplifying. We can nod sympathetically when shown the charts that graph our use of resources against the rest of the world's. We even can start recycling and feel good about it. But the real issues get addressed when we take out our checkbooks—the bottom line, so to speak.

We can take care of overcrowded schedules, out of control to-do lists, cluttered closets, noisy environments, and all the other trappings that accompany a broken lifestyle. Those are the superficial wounds. The life-threatening blow comes when the dollar amount needs filling in. That one hurts. Is this really the life we want to threaten? Don't feel embarrassed if, at a point like this, you suddenly want to start screaming, "But it's mine, mine, all of it mine!" It's taken us a long time to address the issue of the checkbook. We're still working on it.

We've been given a ten percent guideline. Guidelines are helpful. They need not become burdensome unless we allow them to. They are, on the other hand, limiting, as if reaching ten percent in our giving means we've plateaued—reached the amount at which we can go no higher. You know as well as we do that it's all relative.

Simplicity does not count numbers or percentages. It simply allows people to respond as they are able and willing, once credit balances are in check, and mortgages within manageable amounts. Once we have freed up encumbered resources we have many choices. It's a matter of following. Listening to the call once again. Learning to live with what we hear. Serving one God instead of many.

**SCRIPTURE:** 2 Corinthians 9:6-15

> *Each man should give what he has decided in his heart to give, not reluctantly or under compulsion, for God loves a cheerful giver.* **2 COR. 9:7 (NIV)**

**ACTION IDEA:**

This week, if only for one week, give to your church community one-tenth of your week's income as a tithe. Don't get all hot and bothered over whether to give one-tenth of your gross income or your net income; just do it. This once. And then, if it feels right . . . , keep doing it.

**JOURNALING:**

You likely will get two distinctly different feelings from two very different scenarios:

1. Imagine how you'd feel if you'd worked hard all week to scrape out what is barely a living, then be told you *had* to give ten percent of that income to others.

2. Now imagine that you have inherited the equivalent of a week's income and you may keep ninety percent of that total, giving just ten percent to meet the needs of others.

How would it change your understanding of tithing if you spent time dwelling on the fact that all good things in our lives—including our ability to earn an income—come from God? And we get to keep ninety percent of the benefit from all that giftedness!

## DAY SIX—Torn between Two Loves

*I search my heart—I search, and find no faith.*
*Hidden he may be in its many folds—*
*I see him not revealed in all the world*
*Duty's firm shape thins to a misty wraith.*
*No good seems likely. To and fro I am hurled.*
*I have to stay. Only obedience holds—*
*I haste, I rise, I do the thing he saith.*

George MacDonald, *Diary of an Old Soul*

A fifteen-year-old girl expressed it best.

"I feel like I'm being pulled by two horses going in different directions," she lamented one day in counseling. "One pulls me toward what I know is right. The other horse pulls me where I know I shouldn't go. I'm in the middle, needing to make a choice or be torn in two."

It is a human condition, this ambivalence. We search our hearts. No good seems likely. Paul expressed this same struggle in the Scripture for today. Which way to go? Whom will I serve? These questions have been around a long time.

The inner strength of some of us is amazing. Some people can hold on to their horses for a lifetime, even if they are going in opposite directions. It's a struggle that requires large amounts of energy. Too often the opposing horse wins out. Which way to go? Whom will I serve? It can tear us apart.

Back and forth we are "hurled." A giant tug-of-war between what we know to be "right" and what we are afraid to let go of. We are most to be pitied. Even a child can see how much easier the journey is if the opposing horse is tamed and harnessed with the other—two horses pulling in one direction. It would be an amazing ride, would it not?

Two horses. Harnessed and ready for the journey. Which way to go? Whom will I serve?

**SCRIPTURE:** Romans 7:15

*I do not understand what I do. For what I want to do I do not do, but what I hate I do.* ROM. 7:15 (NIV)

**ACTION IDEA:**

Where in your life have you felt pulled two ways? Think about your time, your family, your friends, your money, your church, your goals, your loyalties. Choose one area and make a decision today, one way or the other. The energy you have used to hold those "horses" together now can be freed for some other area where it's needed.

**JOURNALING:**

For whatever area you choose, give names to your "horses." What are the forces pulling you toward healthy and unhealthy choices? Self-will, self-indulgence, obedience, faithfulness? Naming a problem area takes away some of its power and allows it to be more easily tamed. Talk to your "horses" as you journal today. Include petitions to God for guidance and for strength.

## DAY SEVEN—Idols and Egos

*"Yet I may love thee too, O Lord,*
*Almighty as thou art.*
*For thou hast stooped to ask of me*
*The love of my poor heart."* Frederick Faber

Barbara shares:

*Ask to borrow my pen. No problem. Ask to borrow my husband for a meeting. Only a problem if I haven't seen him very much lately. Ask to borrow some of my time. I can manage it. Ask me for my love. All right, who's asking?*

*This isn't a frivolous kind of love God's asking for. It's the heart kind. The kind that pulses through you, tends to take over, controls you if you don't watch out. This isn't the safe kind of love, like loving chocolate or nice summer days. This love, as unconditional as it is, requires something not easily given: authenticity.*

*What does it mean to love God? It means that we allow God to see us at our lowest. We know that. That's what makes it so difficult. No one is supposed to know how low we can go. It's dark down there. Shadowy. As much as I possess the good, I also possess evil. It's a human condition. Terminal, they say.*

*Loving God means I have to be my real self. No false images. Golden calves. Stony statues. God knows it's all a last-ditch attempt to make things appear more perfect than they are. Idols and egos. It's all the same.*

*You're asking for my heart, Lord. My first inclination is to write in some conditions. Limit the love. Reserve the right to call my own shots. Keep playing a part written and directed by me. Allow God to love part of me, the part that looks and acts nice. But that's not heart love. That's not what God's asking here. So what are my options?*

*I always could go on trying to pretend I'm something I'm not.*

**SCRIPTURE:** 1 John 3:1, 4:19

*We love because he first loved us.* **1 JOHN 4:19 (NIV)**

**ACTION IDEA:**

Memorize one of today's Bible verses. Try to bring it to mind every time you have a pause in your day. Stoplights were made for moments like these.

**JOURNALING:**

Today, list the "idols" that you keep in the dark parts of your life. What occupies your thoughts? Where are you still quite self-centered? What elements of your personality cause you and other people damage? Where would you not like God to dwell? Take your time on this. Ask God to bring light into the dark areas of your life, not to judge but to help you face and disarm them. Watch these idols go tumbling to the floor. Repenting allows us to love God more authentically. No holds barred.

This also is the end of week four, a week when you have decluttered, thrown out some of the "junk" of your life, tamed some hassles, and drawn a bead on things that really matter. Did the action ideas pinch a bit harder when we dealt with money? With your over-scheduled schedule? Take note of the places where your reaction is strongest; they are fruitful territory.

It is not enough just to get rid of things that complicate our lives. We also need to embrace some of the gifts that accompany our newfound freedom and simplicity. You're ready for week five.

# CHAPTER 8

# WEEK FIVE—Opening the Gifts

## DAY ONE—Life Attack

*"On the down days, it's just humility, common sense, and patience that get you through the day."* Ben Burdt

When Ben Burdt was in his forties he had a heart attack. It changed his life. He dropped weight, never took an elevator again, began to ride his bike wherever he could. On his eightieth birthday he ran the Great Wall of China. No kidding.

Ben is the kind of person you want to be around. He doesn't take himself or you too seriously. He knows what it takes to get you through the day. He knows we all struggle sometimes. It's all part of life and nothing to fear.

If one wants to learn a lesson in humility, Ben is not a bad example. He took charge of his life. He made some changes and lives happily with the consequences. He hasn't ever done a "great" thing, although he has done many small things in a great way. He loves easily.

Love keeps us humble. It takes the focus off ourselves and directs it back at others. A lot of people's unhappiness comes from the fact that they have forgotten how to love. They focus in on their own feelings, discomforts, and anger. They puff themselves up, expecting a little gratitude for all they do. Do we ever get enough gratitude? So we scowl and keep our eyes down and wonder why our days are weighted and without joy.

The longing for a simpler life is like having a "life attack" rather than a heart attack. We all can benefit from Ben Burdt's example. Drop some of the extra "weight" we have collected along the way. Slow our pace whenever possible. Look out for the person next to us. We may not run the Great Wall of China when we are eighty, but we certainly will enjoy the journey a lot more.

**SCRIPTURE:** Matthew 5:3-12

*Blessed are the peacemakers, for they will be called sons of God.*

MATT. 5:9 (NIV)

**ACTION IDEA:**

Think of a person who gives you peace. Call that person on the phone and spend some time talking with him or her. Tell that person about your goals for simplicity in your life and that this week the theme is gifts and thankfulness. Express your thanks for the gift of peace.

**JOURNALING:**

Reflect on the Scripture portion above commonly called "the Beatitudes." Stop and remain in silence after each verse. How might these Scriptures be directed into your own life? What do they say to you about your relationship with the rest of the world? Claim one of the "Beatitudes" for the day. Reflect upon it several times throughout the day.

## DAY TWO—Big Plans

*"At that point in life where your talent meets the needs of the world, that is where God wants you to be."*

Albert Schweitzer

As young people, we dream dreams about what God might do with the great talents God has given us. We dream big of how we will conquer the world's injustices, how we will win friends and influence people. We write inspiring stories in our hearts, sing stirring melodies, and wonder when and how God will use us in the future.

Then the future comes. Some of the "youthfulness" wears off the dreams. And yet we wait for that moment when God really will use us. Really kick in with that big plan, the one that changes things, makes a "mark in the world." We wait.

Don't dismiss one if you primarily do the other. Both are valuable. Write your reflections in your journal.

## DAY SEVEN—Walking on Water

> *"The way of simplicity is open for everyone. But it requires 'all' of us. Total attentiveness. If we play around with it, the result will be the same as with every game: when it's over 'real life' is the same. There is no transformation. The same dull suffering and delusion is still there."*
>
> Tilden Edwards, *Living Simply Through the Day*, p. 233

Six weeks. It's a beginning. Long enough to begin to sense the real adventure out there. Long enough to know if "this one's for you."

What ground have we covered? We stopped to listen. We learned how to identify God's voice in unusual places, even in our discomfort. We confronted lions and knocked down idols. We learned to serve one God instead of many. We uncovered some of our gifts and learned to share those gifts again. We found meaning by what we don't possess rather than by what we have. Not bad for a first attempt. We hope you have been blessed in this undertaking.

These six weeks have not been offered as a set of guidelines to follow or new commandments to keep. We would not be that brash. There is always the possibility that after the initial yearnings for simplicity we yawn, stretch back, and say, "That was nice" and continue on our way. There is no graduation ceremony, moving us from one way of life into another. Simplicity will not be possessed. It remains, as ever, a calling available to all who hear, but owned by no one.

If simplicity can be anything, let it be a pilgrimage, traveled alone or with others. A pilgrimage made up of small choices, daily choices that affect all aspects of our lives. There is no line dividing personal faith and social action. Jesus saw it as one. It would be unwise to try and divide them.

Simplicity is not a plan to save the world, although it could have some large consequences on the way things are. But we walk this journey. One step at a time. Patiently waiting for the next call. Keep listening. Answer when you are able.

**SCRIPTURE:** Philippians 1:6

> *Being confident of this, that he who began a good work in you will carry it on to completion until the day of Christ Jesus.*
>
> PHIL. 1:6 (NIV)

**ACTION IDEA:**

Today, this last day of your six-week commitment, commit yourself to two or three acts of simplicity and pledge to do them on a daily basis. Members of a loosely formed community called "The Order of Saints Martin and Theresa" write in their journals daily, wear a paper clip symbolizing nonviolence, and take daily walks. You might choose to continue Bible reading and writing in your journal, and then add a third action that feels just right for you.

**JOURNALING:**

This brings us to the end of our six-week journey. Sit in silence for several minutes and let the thought roll over you that you have been becoming more acquainted with God's gift of simplicity for some time now. What began as a lifestyle experiment has led to steady, healthy habits. If you have been reading the suggested Scriptures regularly and journaling your thoughts, as well as taking active steps on the journey toward a simpler lifestyle, you have made a good start. You are grooved into habits that will not easily disappear. Treasure the progress you have made and the new priorities you have forged.

Direct a special word of thanks to God in prose or poetry for this journey and then move on to the next chapter, which will help you evaluate and reflect even more on your journey, as well as look ahead to possible journeys in your future.

# CHAPTER 10

# Photo Albums and Itineraries

*We too take ship, O soul*
*Joyous we too launch out on trackless seas . . .*
*Caroling free, singing our song of God,*
*Chanting our chant of pleasant exploration . . .*
*Sail forth—steer for the deep waters only,*
*Reckless, O soul, exploring, I with thee, and thou with me,*
*For we are bound where the mariner has not yet dared to go,*
*And we will risk the ship, ourselves and all.*

*O my brave soul!*
*O farther, farther sail!*
*O daring joy but safe! are they not all the seas of God?*
*O farther, farther, farther sail.*

"Be Not Afraid" by Walt Whitman

By God's grace you have braved the journey toward the distant shores called "Simplicity." We all have yet to arrive at that destination—we have not yet fully embraced the gift that God offers—but perhaps in the past six weeks your lifestyle has become more thoughtful, more intentional, more focused, simpler.

In this chapter you will find two meaningful ways to reflect on your recent journey toward simplicity: (1) You will construct a "photo album" of memories from your journey thus far, and (2) you will fill out an "itinerary" anticipating your continuing journey.

### Your "Photo Album"

Use the spaces provided to jot or sketch memories of how your life has changed in the past six weeks:

- How is your life different from what it was six weeks ago?

- What were the most significant hindrances as you traveled along your journey?

- Did you pick up any passengers along the way? Did anyone close to you express interest or curiosity in the lifestyle changes they heard you talking about or that they observed in you?

- Did the journey lead you out of complexity into greater simplicity? Or does the fact that you have been facing life's realities in a new way make things less simple?

- As you review your journal entries, what trends or growth can you observe?

### Your Itinerary

The journey toward a simpler lifestyle is more like moving to a new home than going on a vacation. Hopefully, you are not going to return to the place from which you set out six weeks ago.

Indeed, the journey continues every minute of your life. So where to now? Use the spaces provided to jot down or sketch an itinerary for your further journeys toward a simpler, more integrated lifestyle:

- What are you longing for most in your lifestyle that you have yet to achieve? Take another look at the lifestyle survey. Are there still some areas to work on? Also read the section "A Look Back, a Look Ahead," on page 112.

- Is it important for you to be heading toward specific personal goals, or is it more your style to see the journey unfold as you go through each day? If you prefer clearly defined goals, list five or more of the most important directions you want your life to go.

- What Scriptures have caught your attention and will be beacons that light the way for your future lifestyle journeys?

- In what ways can you gently include others in your journey toward a simpler lifestyle?

- Richard Foster writes in *Celebration of Discipline*: "Superficiality is the curse of our age. The doctrine of instant satisfaction is a primary spiritual problem. The desperate need today is not for a greater number of intelligent people, or gifted people, but for deep people" (page 1). In what ways have you found greater depth in your journey toward simplicity, and in what ways are you still wanting to steer for the "deep waters?"

## A Look Back, a Look Ahead

Throughout these six weeks, many of the action ideas not only were helpful for a given day but also had the potential of continued use. Here is a sampling of ideas that you might want to keep on doing as you plan ways to live your simpler life.

- Deal with unresolved conflicts, hurts, anger, and other emotional baggage (Week One, Day Three).
- Make the sign of the cross or some other symbolic physical action to remember God (Week One, Day Six).
- Chart your days to watch for patterns and to help you make healthy changes (Week Two, Day One).
- Continue to make confession of your brokenness as needed and to claim God's power to heal it (Week Two, Day Four).
- Evaluate your time commitments, using the guidelines given (Week Two, Day Six).
- Stay home five nights out of seven; setting aside time for family and friends (Week Three, Day One).
- Get acquainted with people different from yourself; become involved in their lives (Week Three, Day Two).
- Do justice with issues that matter to you; let your voice be heard (Week Three, Day Three).
- Laugh; take a break from the seriousness of life (Week Three, Day Six).
- Declutter some part of your home—closet, pantry, garage, whatever (Week Four, Day One).
- Watch to see where you are being pulled two ways; make decisions to resolve the conflicting pulls (Week Four, Day Six).
- See Christ in the people around you, treat them respectfully, thank God for them (Week Five, Day Two).
- Spend time outdoors, enjoying nature, getting involved in ways to care for God's creation (Week Five, Day Five).
- Keep Sunday as a real day of rest; find ways to have little sabbaths during busy times (Week Five, Day Six).
- Keep in touch with people whose lives seem dark from loneliness, illness, or other needs (Week Six, Day Three).
- Write letters or call government officials and decision-makers about issues that matter to you (Week Six, Day Four).

- Carry a small cross, using it as a reminder of your intention to follow Christ (Week Six, Day Six).
- Continue to do three actions of your choice each day as a reminder of your goal to live a simpler life (Week Six, Day Seven).

## Farewell

We are grateful to have had you for a traveling companion. As we've written this book, we have prayed for you regularly and sought to guide you into places of the heart where the Holy Spirit has done the best work in us. Where we have failed to anticipate your needs or your questions, please forgive us. Where we have helped you gain a new perspective and a new joy in following Jesus Christ, we must give the praise to God for moving our own hearts into greater health and giving us a love of sharing the life-giving movement of the Holy Spirit with others through our writing.

Share your journey toward simplicity *gently* with others. As the Danish philosopher and theologian Søren Kierkegaard was fond of pointing out, there usually are two ditches into which a person may fall. In this case, one ditch would be to set up your own journey as a mandate for others. God has given us quite enough laws to govern our behavior, thank you very much. But the other ditch, into which we do not want to fall, would be to fail to share the joy and freedom that comes from a life centered on things that are simply of enduring and eternal importance.

A world of people around us are desperately ill in the spirit and in need of a journey to other shores and fairer climes. They don't need simplicity, per se. They need Jesus Christ. For those who are called by Jesus and given the gift of longing for a better life, greater simplicity will follow.

Walk gently in your new awarenesses and good intentions. People near to you have been used to you the "old" way and may resist changes, not only in themselves, but also in you. But persist, knowing that God has given you something very precious. As Peter wrote, "Who is going to harm you if you are eager to do good? But even if you should suffer for what is right, you are blessed. 'Do not fear what they fear; do not be frightened.' But in your hearts, set apart Christ as Lord. Always be prepared to give an answer to everyone who asks you to give the reason for the hope that you have. But do this with gentleness and respect" (1 Peter 3:13-15, NIV).

**APPENDIX**

# Using This Book in a Small Group

Lifestyle journeys are more fun and potentially more effective and enduring when they are shared with other people. As professional public school and church educators, we feel *Six Weeks to a Simpler Lifestyle* would be an especially good choice to use in small-group study and discussion.

Use this book for an adult education class on a Sunday morning, with an adult reading group on a weekday over lunch or in the evening, or as a point of focus among friends of various backgrounds in a home study group. We've tried to make it a personal journey for each reader, but one that also can be shared in a mixed group of single and/or married people.

A seven-week commitment to study *Six Weeks to a Simpler Lifestyle* would be ideal. The first session could be used to discuss the introduction and Chapters 1–3. Then each of the remaining six sessions could follow one of the weeks of assigned readings, action ideas, and journaling found in Chapters 4–9. The seventh session also would include some personal reflection as generated from the material in Chapter 10.

*Six Weeks to a Simpler Lifestle* also could be used during a weekend retreat with the understanding that participants would journey through the book on their own during the six weeks *prior* to attending the retreat. The process of mutual study and support contained in this appendix could be used during seven one-hour sessions over a single weekend: Session 1 Friday evening, Sessions 2 and 3 Saturday morning, Session 4 right after lunch, Session 5 late Saturday afternoon, after a few hours of free time, Session 6 Saturday evening, and Session

7 Sunday morning, prior to a closing worship that centers around some of the key Scriptures presented in the book.

Participants should be given personal copies of *Six Weeks to a Simpler Lifestyle* a week before the first session, if possible, so each will have read through Chapter 3 before the group gathers for the first time. Make sure they take and score the lifestyle survey found in Chapter 2 before the first session. Support your local Christian bookstore by purchasing the books there or, if necessary, you may order directly from Augsburg Fortress Publishers by calling, toll free, 1–800–328–4648.

Having a single discussion leader for all the sessions would be helpful, though not absolutely necessary. That person will: (1) help initiate and move the conversation along, (2) bring the group back on track if it strays too far for too long, (3) call for participation by others if one person monopolizes the discussion, (4) field questions and enlist the help of others in responding, and (5) bring each session to a timely conclusion.

## SESSION ONE: (50–60 minutes)

After the group has gathered, invite members to share for one minute each who they are and why the topic of *Six Weeks to a Simpler Lifestyle* appeals to them. Then lead the group as you discuss the questions for Session 1.

1. What is your background with the topic of simplicity? Have you read the authors' previous book, *'Tis a Gift to Be Simple: Embracing the Freedom of Living with Less*, or other books or articles on the subject?
2. What are some recent "salty" experiences you've had that made you "thirsty" for some changes in your lifestyle?
3. What are some of the pressures in your community that are causing people to get overwhelmed, overextended, and overly complex?
4. Meet in groups of two or three and take about ten minutes to share results of the lifestyle survey from Chapter 2, pages 18–24. You may want to share what you have learned from the survey, especially in which area or areas you find you are longing for change.

5. Have you had experience keeping a diary or personal journal? If so, share with the others how the process helped you.
6. The Bible promises that God is able to "make all things new." Why do you have reason to believe this is really true? Do you have a personal story of a time when God created something fresh and new within you?

Close with a minute of silence during which time participants are encouraged to thank God for the other members of the discussion group.

Ask participants to begin the first week process (Chapter 4) within the next 24 hours and come to the next session ready to discuss what happened during week one. Encourage them not to bypass the chance to keep a journal; they may share as much or as little of their journal writing as they like, but it will be an important component of their learning.

## SESSION TWO (50–60 minutes)

As an introduction to this session, ask participants to describe briefly someone who is likely to support their longings for a simpler lifestyle. Then discuss the questions based on week 1 in Chapter 4, "Getting a Quick Start" and the participants' journal entries.

1. What is the benefit of an action/reflection model of lifestyle change?
2. Were you tempted to take any shortcuts during this first week of the journey toward a simpler lifestyle? Did you feel like ignoring some suggestions like keeping a journal?
3. When have you had an experience that hurt "good," one that caused you to seek a healthier lifestyle?
4. What did you find worthy of your lamenting on day two? Were you also able to see something to thank God for?
5. What kinds of emotional "baggage" will you need to deal with in order to be more freed up to make lifestyle changes in the upcoming weeks?
6. Does the thought that you might choose to give something up later in order to gain greater simplicity bother you? Why or why not?

7. What steps have you taken recently (or would like to take) to simplify your time commitments?
8. What (and who) will help you to be persistent in re-prioritizing and living out the changes you long for?

Close with a minute of silence during which time participants are encouraged to offer God their good intentions and ask God for guidance and strength.

The assignment for the next session is to work through week 2 in Chapter 5 on the subject of listening.

## SESSION THREE (50–60 minutes)

For an opening, ask participants to share how important it is to experience the "peace that passes understanding." Then point out that the peace promised in Philippians occurs only in a relationship of prayer with God. Read Phil. 4:6-7. This session's discussion is based on week 2 in Chapter 5, "Listening," and the participants' journal entries.

1. What feelings have you noticed as major patterns in your life in recent days and weeks? What did charting your days show you? What changes are you considering?
2. Do you sense a "calling" to a life of greater simplicity? If so, in what ways did that calling come to you?
3. In groups of two or three, spend some time talking about your brokenness (see day 4). Some people may choose not to share. Listeners are to respect the confidential and holy nature of this sharing.
4. What have you done and what more can you do to slow the pace of your life? What tasks or commitments did you draw Xs through?
5. Again, in groups of two or three, share an area of your life where you know you need to change (refer to the lifestyle survey) but you just haven't gotten around to it. After hearing each person's confession, the rest are to say, kindly but firmly, "Just stop."
6. What image or phrase have you found that brings focus and direction to your life?

7. Two weeks into your journey, what concerns and questions do you have about the study or discussion?

In closing, allow a minute of silence during which time people are to remember any progress they are making and thank God for the prompting to seek a simpler lifestyle. The assignment for the next session is to work through Chapter 6 on how to deal with struggles.

## SESSION FOUR (50–60 minutes)

Invite participants to open the session by recalling a song or hymn that gets them through struggles. Ask them if they are willing to sing or whistle a verse, or to show the words. Then discuss the questions based on week 3, Chapter 6, "Naming the Struggles," and their journal entries.

1. Who in your community are the "haves" and who are the "have-nots?" How do people keep the have-nots at a distance? What can you learn from the have-nots?
2. What action idea(s) have you found that you wanted to avoid? Why the avoidance? Which topics from the lifestyle survey are the hardest to work on?
3. Time out! The subject of changing lifestyles is in danger of getting too intense at times. Who has heard a good joke recently that could lighten things up a bit? What can you do in your daily routines that lifts your spirits and lightens you up? When do you laugh?
4. When have you gone through a time that seemed serious at first but later you found you could laugh at yourself?
5. What issues exist in your community that beg for people to work for justice? What do you have to offer to these issues? Which ones are priorities for you?
6. At the midway point in this six-week process, what is the best thing you are getting from the book and from the group?

In closing, share once again a minute of silence, this time praying for others who have a special need for help from you and perhaps others in your discussion group. The assignment for next week is to be ready to discuss week 4 in Chapter 7, "Serving Only God."

## SESSION FIVE (50–60 minutes)

To open the session, read responsively Psalm 96 (two groups read every other verse or half verse). You may want to have photocopies available so they all are reading from the same version of the Bible. Then discuss the following questions based on week 4, Chapter 7, "Serving Only God."

1. Where has your life clamored for "decluttering?" What have you done about it?
2. What are some areas in which you have had disagreements with a loved one on what is a "want" and what is a "need?" What have you done to resolve this conflict?
3. Besides meeting your bodily needs, what are the two most important things you do? Do you do them because you have to or because you want to, or both?
4. How easy is it for you to "do nothing" (day 4)? What is behind the compulsion that many of us have to keep doing *something*?
5. Do you enjoy or avoid solitude? Think about the difference between solitude and loneliness. You might want to enjoy five minutes of uninterrupted silence right now to use in any way you see fit (move around, sit, read, pray). Afterwards, discuss how comfortable you felt.
6. In what ways do you put your money where your mouth is in the things you consider important? What are some of your priorities each month once the rent or mortgage payment has been paid?
7. What are some of the "horses" that threaten to pull you in two different directions? Here are three examples: 1. Time—wanting to get things accomplished and wanting to have time to rest and reflect. 2. Emotions—liking so many people and so many activities but having too little time. 3. God—waiting for, depending on God and doing things without God, on your own.

Close with a minute of silence during which time participants may offer to God the "idols" that divide their loyalty to

God. Prepare for next week by studying and following the process for week 5 in Chapter 8, "Opening the Gifts."

## SESSION SIX (50–60 minutes)

Open by asking participants to describe a person sixty-five years of age or older who has healthy priorities. Why do you think this person is this way? Then discuss the questions based on week 5, Chapter 8, "Opening the Gifts," and their journal entries.

1. Which of the Beatitudes in Matt. 5:3-12 is your favorite? Why?
2. What dreams of grandeur have you had to give up as you've gotten older? Was this humbling experience difficult for you?
3. Whom do you know who has the gift of hospitality?
4. Name two things you do with your time that are gifts to others. Name two things others do that are gifts to you.
5. Nature is a perfect place to go to reevaluate our lives. How do you keep in touch with nature? What more can you do?
6. What can you do to give yourself Sabbath rests even on busy days? What can you do, to keep each Sunday more of a sabbath than they have been?
7. At the end of your fifth week in this six-week process on the path to a simpler lifestyle, what negative elements have you begun to remove from your life? What positive elements have you added? Why is it important to do some of each?

Close with a minute of silence during which time you don't do anything but listen. At times there are just too many words, and we need some Sabbath silence for our tongues and our minds as well.

Prepare for the next session by working through week 6, Chapter 9, "Blessed to Be a Blessing," and chapter 10, "Photo Albums and Itineraries."

## SESSION SEVEN (50–60 minutes)

Open this final session by asking participants to share what they have appreciated most about the time spent with the other participants. Then discuss the questions based on week 6 in Chapter 9 and Chapter 10, along with journal entries.

1. Describe a time when Jesus Christ seemed most real and powerful to you.
2. How difficult is it for you to ask other people for help? Do you find it any easier to ask God for help?
3. In groups of two or three, share (as much as you are willing) some of the dark areas of your life, as identified on day 3.
4. Would you rather bake a pie or send a letter to a government official? Which is more important? Why? What other actions are important?
5. Why is it good to plant trees and otherwise be in touch with the earth and growing things? What is being done in your community to care for the earth? How can you help?
6. Are you a leader or a follower, spiritually? Are you one at times and the other at other times? What are those times?
7. In groups of two or three share, as Chapter 10 directs, some of your memories of the last six weeks and your plans for a continuing journey on the path toward a simpler lifestyle.

In concluding this final session, have the participants join hands and share a minute of silence, followed by everybody praying aloud the Lord's Prayer.

Depart in God's peace.

# ANNOTATED BIBLIOGRAPHY

Crean, David, et al., eds. *Living Simply: An Examination of Christian Lifestyles*. New York: The Seabury Press, 1981. A study guide by an ecumenical collection of authors who address the problems of dwindling world resources and how simpler lifestyles can help.

DeGrote-Sorensen, Barbara and Sorensen, David. *'Tis a Gift to Be Simple: Embracing the Freedom of Living with Less*. Minneapolis: Augsburg Fortress, 1992. If the book you have in your hands is a "how-to" invitation to simplicity, then our first book on this topic is the "why-to" book. Explores personal, social, and biblical motivations for making lifestyle changes.

Edwards, Tilden. *Living Simply Through the Day: Spiritual Survival in a Complex Age*. New York: Paulist Press, 1977. Helps the reader view simplicity through the "windows" of waking, praying, relating, serving, eating, playing, aching, and sleeping.

Elgin, Duane. *Voluntary Simplicity: Toward a Way of Life that Is Outwardly Simple, Inwardly Rich*. New York: William Morrow and Company, 1981. A personal and global look at the opportunity simpler living gives for a more balanced future.

Finnerty, Adam Daniel. *No More Plastic Jesus*. Maryknoll: Orbis, 6th printing, 1987. A call to integrity between lifestyle principles and practice on a global scale.

Foster, Richard J. *Celebration of Discipline: The Path to Spiritual Growth*. New York: Harper & Row, 1978. A modern "spiritual classic" already and a personal favorite of ours, this book contains sections on the inner, outer, and corporate disciplines, including a chapter on simplicity.

Foster, Richard J. *Freedom of Simplicity.* San Francisco: HarperSanFrancisco, 1981. Typical Foster: top-notch biblical work and research, deft insights, gives meaning to your own personal examples.

Hart, Archibald D. *The Hidden Link Between Adrenalin and Stress.* Dallas: Word Publishing, 1991. A practical guide to identifying and healing the "hurry sickness" caused by the body's reaction to stress.

Heloise. *Hints For A Healthy Planet.* New York: Perigee Books, 1990. Helps for a simpler lifestyle don't have to come only from Christian sources. This little book contains lots of specific ideas that get one in the mood to live a more integrated life for the benefit of all.

Kelsey, Morton T. *Adventure Inward: Christian Growth through Personal Journal Writing.* Minneapolis: Augsburg Publishing House, 1980. A thorough look at the whys, the hows and the how-nots of keeping a personal journal.

Kiekegaard, Søren. *Purity of Heart Is to Will One Thing.* New York: Harper & Row, 1938. Simplicity is a matter of the inner heart as well as of outward lifestyle. This is a book on motivations and priorities; challenging but rewarding reading for the theologically minded.

Klug, Ronald. *How to Keep a Spiritual Journal.* Minneapolis: Augsburg Fortress, 1993. An excellent, practical, and comprehensive guide to inner growth and personal discovery through keeping a personal spiritual journal.

Longacre, Doris Janzen. *Living More with Less.* Scottdale: Herald Press, 1980. A classic on the subject of voluntary simplicity and its benefits.

McGinnis, Alan Loy. *The Power of Optimism.* New York: Harper & Row, 1990. A good book to help the process toward a simpler lifestyle be a positive experience rather than a series of losses and setbacks.

Ruggiero, Vincent Ryan. *Good Habits: Self-Improvement for the 1990s.* Louisville: Westminster/John Knox Press, 1991. A helpful, forward-looking book with many concrete examples of people who develop good habits.

Schaef, Anne Wilson. *When Society Becomes an Addict.* New York: Harper & Row, 1987. A somewhat controversial but significant book revealing some of our society's addictive motivations that get us into lifestyle troubles.

Shames, Laurence. *The Hunger for More: Searching for Values in an Age of Greed*. New York: Random House, 1989. An excellent exposé of our society's tendency toward greed by a highly competent secular writer.

Talbot, John Michael with Dan O'Neill. *Simplicity*. Ann Arbor: Redeemer Books, 1991. A good overview with practical helps from a Roman Catholic musician's perspective on inner spirituality and exterior simplicity.

Thoreau, Henry David. *Walden*. New York: Barnes & Noble, 1993. A classic book on the two-year experiment of Thoreau to live a simpler life on Walden Pond. A nice balance to this book—adding Christian spirituality—might be Kierkegaard's *Purity of Heart Is to Will One Thing* which deals with inner simplicity of motivations.

Van Klompenburg, Carol. *What To Do When You Can't Do It All*. Minneapolis: Augsburg Publishing House, 1989. An excellent guide to help sift through unrealistic expectations on the way to discovering anew the grace of God.

Woodworth, Steve. *52 Ways to Simplify Your Life*. Nashville: Thomas Nelson Publishers, 1993. A helpful buckshot approach to simplifying one's lifestyle that includes many personal insights and calls to action.

Ziegler, Edward K. *Simple Living*. Elgin: The Brethren Press, 1974. Draws contemporary insights from the concept and practice of simple living taught through the years by the Church of the Brethren.